Brussels to Beirut to Bali

*The 1958 World Travels of
Four Girls in a Second-Hand Chevy*

PUBLISHED April 2015

ISBN 978-0-9635018-9-9

EDITORIAL SERVICES David A. Wilk

ART DIRECTION Danielle Kent

PRODUCTION Layout & Design: Anna Lafferty
Lafferty Design Plus, Santa Barbara, CA

PUBLISHER KIERAN PUBLISHING COMPANY
*Interesting Books that Inform, Inspire,
Educate & Entertain*

P.O. BOX 3683
Santa Barbara, California 93130

Brussels to Beirut to Bali

The 1958 World Travels of
Four Girls in a Second-Hand Chevy

Dana Matthaei Kent

Kieran Publishing Company

Chapter Photos - Descriptions

Preface: *Expo '58 logo designed by Lucien De Roeck was every where in Brussels*

1. *My granddaughter Sophie*

2. *An original painting of the ocean liner,* **SS America with Parked Cars**, *painted by Wayne Mazzotta, 2009*

3. *At my news desk at the Morristown Daily Record*

4. *The Atomium, symbol of the Brussels World's Fair*

5. *My passport which contains two long foldout extensions*

6. *Our 1953 Chevy packed to go with Gloria, Jane and Sue*

7. *Max, his sister and her child in Rome*

8. *Sue, Gloria and Jane with new friends in Yugoslavia*

9. *Our Chevy parked in Zagreb*

10. *On bridge in Belgrade*

11. *A shepherd and his flock crossing the road in Greece*

12. *The Parthenon in Athens*

13. *Our Chevy being loaded onto the ship in Piraeus*

14. *I am with members of Sadat's family at their home in Ankara*

15. *A camel caravan crossing the road in Turkey*

16. *Dancing with Adnan in Damascus*

17. *Traveling from Damascus to Beirut*

18. *Jane and I with our friend the border guard*

19. *A rainy day in Amman with Gloria, me and Jane*

20. *Fixing our car outside of Bethlehem*

21. *The Walls of Jericho*

22. *A letter to my mother*

23. *Landing at the Kabul Airport*

24. *A horse drawn cart in Lahore*

25. *Sue, Jane, me and Gloria reunited in New Dehli*

26. *Gloria with Dr. Hall in Ajmer*

27. *Transportation options in Jaipur*

28. *The Taj Mahal*

29. *On the shore of the Ganges*

30. *Stewart, Gloria, Jane and me with friend in Calcutta*

31. *Temple of the Dawn in Bangkok*

32. *Our hostesses in Kuala Lumpur*

33. *The Countess and her friend in Singapore*

34. *A vender carrying his wares in Jakarta*

35. *The terraced rice paddies of Indonesia*

36. *Our mode of transportation in Eastern Java*

37. *The men's chorus at the Monkey Dance*

38. *The culprit*

39. *The USS President Wilson passing under the Golden Gate Bridge*

Acknowledgements

I want to thank my daughter Dani who has been my tech expert, part time editor, sounding board and art director. In her great patience she has been an invaluable resource to me. I would also like to thank David Wilk who encouraged me to become a storyteller rather than a reporter. And my many thanks to my husband Dave who has supported me throughout these many years.

Most of the photos used in the chapter heads are Minox prints which I took along the way. Some of the other photos were publicity photos taken by various sources.

After about fifty years I have reunited with Sue, one of my fellow travelers. I visited her in her northern California home and much to my delight she is the same bright, interesting and witty person that she was in the days when we travelled together.

In anticipation of my visit she sent someone into her attic to retrieve a document she had written during our travels which describes the last part of our journey. Sue has written an account which has enhanced my memory and given me another perspective on our adventure. I have incorporated some of her accounts in the last part of my story and thank her for her time and contribution to this project.

Preface

Everyone who came to Expo 58 that summer came to see the world in a nutshell. The World's Fair took place in Brussels, Belgium and offered a bird's eye view of the world as each participating country put its best foot forward in an exhibit. Four of us young women left there with a lot of blind determination and would need all the luck a pack of poor little lambs could hope for as we traveled home around the world.

Breezing from pavilion to pavilion, having lunch in the USSR and dinner in Japan, our lives were packed full of living, laughing and learning to get along with people who were different from the ones we had known all of our lives. Our remarkable experience at the World's Fair was, perhaps, the answer to the question we were most frequently asked about our subsequent adventure: "Why are you making a trip around the world?"

The year was 1958 and I was among a group of young Americans selected to represent our country as guides at the World's Fair in Belgium. I and many of my fellow guides came to Brussels hoping to find something. Most of us not only

failed to find it but also failed to find out why we were searching in the first place.

Some continued the search in Europe, some went home. I
and three other American girls left at the close of the Fair to
attempt an ambitious seven-month journey around the world.
We traveled 22,000 miles and learned at least wherein our
answers lay.

The deep feeling for, the appreciation and the complete
trust we placed in the friends we met cannot be expressed.
Thanks are not enough for the poor family in Greece who gave
us their last bit of coffee or for the truck driver who worked
on our car for three hours, having been awake and working for
72 hours. The only true reward was the feeling in our hearts…
and I hope in the hearts of all the friends we made. Our completely honest search began and ended with individuals.

If only everyone could be as lucky as we were, war would
be a thing of the past.

Our thanks go out as well to those who discouraged and for-
bade us to make the trip. If we had taken their advice, we might
have continued living in fear of the other peoples of this world.

I was not present when the girls decided to plan the trip. It
was over breakfast one morning when these great forces met.
Gloria had traveled through Europe countless times; Sue was
eager to meet up with a suitor in Damascus; and Jane had been
plotting for months to find a way to get to Indonesia where
her parents had recently relocated.

The fourth member of the original group knew the King
of Bora Bora and was sure that she could get a ride home if
she could make it that far.

I did not know any kings but was very anxious to meet a
few and asked them to put me on the waiting list.

Two months before the closing of the Fair, where we were
working in the American Pavilion, my number came up —
the King of Bora Bora's friend could not go, so I became the
fourth traveler.

CHAPTER ONE
Letter to Sophie
January 7, 2014

This story about my travels around the world began with a letter to my granddaughter Sophie.

Sophie is as interested in the world today as I was at the same age. She is currently pursuing graduate studies at a prestigious school of international studies.

Fortunately, I kept a very detailed journal and recently uncovered my old trunk full of letters, photographs, news clippings and even a supply list and expense record that I have used to describe this odyssey.

I began my "Dear Sophie" letter by explaining that today's world is so very different from the one I experienced in 1958 that I wanted to share it with her.

My first letter to Sophie began:

Dear Sophie,

I was working as a newspaper reporter for the Newark Evening News in 1958 when I read an article that changed my life. The news item said that the state of New Jersey was hiring young people to work as guides at the upcoming World's Fair in Brussels, Belgium. I knew immediately that this was my opportunity of a lifetime. If I could get that job, I would fulfill my longtime dream of traveling to Europe and they would pay me a salary. After many months of applications, interviews and clearance by the State Department as well as studying to update my skills in a second language, I got the job and was on my way to Brussels.

Little did I know that this was only scratching the surface of the adventures to come and it would lead me on a trip around the world in an amazing journey that began by driving from Brussels to Jerusalem with three other young women. As I look back 56 years later, I still cannot believe that I did it!

Love, Granny

Our Route

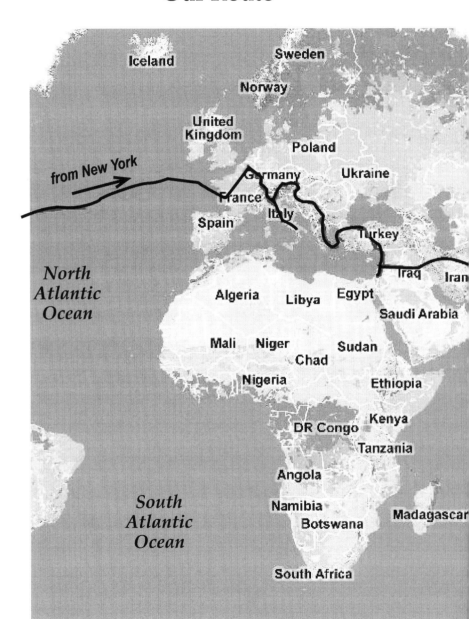

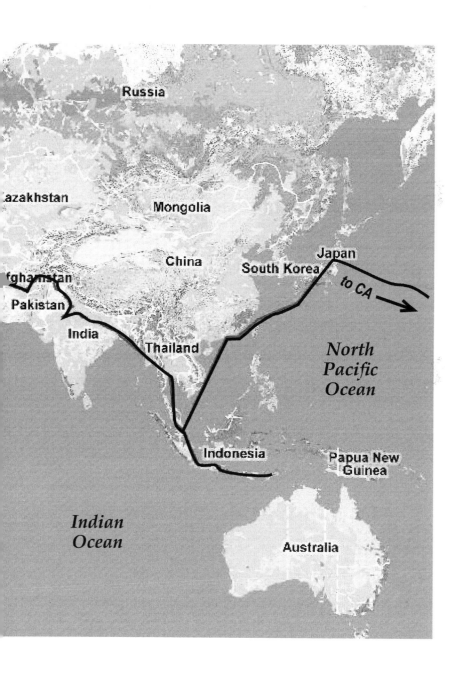

CHAPTER TWO
Sailing from New York
March 28, 1958

My mother, sister, two little nieces and I drove from New Jersey into New York City for my big sendoff on the ocean liner SS America. The massive passenger ship completely wowed me at first sight as it loomed next to the huge terminal building in New York Harbor. Looking up at the two gigantic black smoke stacks perched atop the 10-story hull, I gulped in wonder. What would it feel like to be on board that monster? It looked like a floating city as its 722 feet stretched the length of the pier and out into the Hudson River.

My family and I gathered in the cabin that I would share with a roommate and began a gay farewell party popping the cork of a champagne bottle. Several people had sent bouquets of flowers and boxes of candy. I felt like a celebrity as my little niece said her final goodbye and reminded me to "always put paper on the seat." This became more and more meaningful the further I travelled; I would be facing toilet conditions that were indescribably difficult!

Smoke began to billow from the stacks and a warning bell rang reminding all visitors to leave the ship. I tearfully bade goodbye as I saw them out the door and down the gangplank.

Later I stood on the deck of the ship in my gray sheath dress, high heels and white gloves waving a final farewell to my family and friends. The crew tossed the final line to the dock and I felt as though my ties to everyone I loved and relied upon were being tossed away as well. I was more apprehensive than I had ever been – leaving behind my country, my family and the life I had made for myself. At the same time, my heart was bursting with excitement and anticipation.

What if I became sick? Who would take care of me? What if I did not like Brussels, how could I get back home? Would I be homesick and regret going so far away?

To avoid the queasy feeling in the pit of my stomach I turned my thoughts elsewhere. I decided that I must not dwell on these negative fears; I had to move forward. I took one last look at the Statue of Liberty as we sailed by and realized that the size of that figure was a fitting analogy to the enormity of the unknown future I was facing. My dream had come true: I had been hired by the state of New Jersey to serve as a guide in the American Pavilion of the 1958 Brussels World's Fair. I would be living and working in Europe for the next six months.

As the land slowly faded from sight, I drank in the salty smell of the air. I loved the wind blowing in my face and the wonderful fresh air filling my lungs. I did not want to go inside for fear that it would be too close and confining. I knew I had to begin somewhere but was hesitant to enter that unfamiliar world in which I did not know anyone. Everything seemed strange, as I had never been on an ocean liner before much less been out of the country. I felt completely alone and knew that from now on in I had only myself to rely upon.

I watched the sunlight fade into darkness and left the upper deck to return to my assigned cabin. On entering, I learned that my roommate was as bewildered as I was. "I am Nancy Gore," she said in her warm southern accent. "I live in Tennessee. Where are you from?" Nancy was the sister of Al Gore, who would become vice president to Bill Clinton. Years later, I read in the newspaper that Nancy had married and had a family but sadly died at a young age from lung cancer. I remembered that she was a heavy smoker when I knew her. Her brother Al came within a controversial Supreme Court decision of becoming the 43rd president of the United States instead of George Bush, which would have profoundly changed history.

Nancy and I left our stateroom and climbed the stairway to the main salon for a welcome meeting where we would receive basic instructions and seating assignments for meals. Our leader outlined our schedule for the duration of the crossing.

We would be required to attend a lecture every morning in which we would learn about art history, politics, ecology, agriculture and every other subject about which people would question us as we stood on duty at our exhibits in the United States' pavilion.

The schedule went smoothly for two days as we attended lectures and they measured us for the uniforms we would be wearing for the next six months.

As the third day dawned, I looked out of the porthole and saw white caps splashing on the water. The seas became rougher and rougher as the day wore on and the ship began to pitch and yaw as it forced its way through the growing waves. It became more and more difficult to walk the ship's decks as they pitched forward and rolled from side to side. I felt a tickle in my stomach when the ship descended from its climb to the crest of a monstrous swell and then slid down the backside feeling like an elevator suddenly dropping.

This was the beginning of a major north Atlantic storm and the roughest crossing the ship had experienced in 10 years. By the third day, very few guides attended the morning lecture in the large main ballroom. The weather was formidable: rain and wind lashed at the windows and it became impossible to pry open an outside door. Fortunately, I do not suffer from seasickness so I was able to keep struggling my way along the narrow hallway and up the stairs into the ballroom. I thought it peculiar that I did not see any fellow passengers along the way, but I managed to make it to a chair and settled in.

We were watching an art history slide show presentation beaming from a projector balanced on a small table bolted to the floor. Suddenly the ship violently rolled to the port side, people fell out of their chairs and the table ripped from the floor. It flew across the room along with the slide projector, barely missing several students.

Our instructors told us to return to our cabins immediately and remain there until further notice as a safety precaution. We staggered back along the passageway, barely keeping our footing even though we were clinging to side rails. Word got around that the ship had encountered a rogue wave and rolled over so far that one more degree would have caused it to capsize.

They cancelled the lecture series and all other scheduled events. Once they said we could leave our cabins I anxiously stepped out to discover a surreal scene. The passageways and public rooms were deserted. Even the crew had fallen victim to seasickness and remained in their quarters.

One other male guide and I were the only ones upright as far as we could tell. We sat in the lounge far into the night, had a few brandies and decided that the ship was going to sink. We had both donned our raincoats in case we had to face the elements.

This tense situation persisted for several seemingly endless days. I could only imagine how miserable it was for all of those people who could not even venture out of their cabins. Finally the ocean calmed down enough for most passengers to venture out to the light of day. Nancy was still in her bunk looking green so I convinced her that she should get up, take a shower, and go to breakfast. I assured her that she would feel better. She did as I suggested, sat at her assigned table across from a male guide, and immediately threw up. Nancy returned to her bunk and never left it again until we docked at Le Havre, France.

As the ship entered the English Channel and neared the French dock, I was thrilled with my first sight of Europe. Finally, after seven days of this most difficult and unusual Atlantic crossing, our ship had reached its destination. We arrived a day later than scheduled because the ship slowed to half speed through the turbulent sea. I stood on the deck and gazed enthusiastically at the land. Everything seemed smaller, the cranes loading cargo on ships, the railroad cars and even the rails themselves that were narrow gauge. The cities were older: the small buildings reflected their history and presented a great contrast to America where everything was large, even the cars. The anticipation of exploring a new country caused me to reflect on how I had arrived at this most exciting point in my life.

CHAPTER THREE
The Opportunity

Many of my friends at school had travelled to Europe. I envied their opportunity but knew that my family could not afford to send me on such an adventure.

One morning I was sitting at my desk in the newsroom of the *Newark Evening News* when I read an article describing the upcoming Brussels World's Fair. I suddenly realized that I might just have found my opportunity to explore Europe. The story described how each state would hire guides to work in the U.S. pavilion. These young people were required to speak one other language, to be at least 21 years of age, and to have had at least one year of college.

A thought exploded in my head: this was my solution! If I could get that job, they would pay for my transportation to Europe and I would earn a salary to boot!

I immediately started the process of applying for that much sought-after position. I contacted my French teacher from Kent Place School who agreed to see me each afternoon on my way home from work to revitalize my French speaking abilities. I had studied the language for many years and felt sure that I would be able to pass the required Berlitz test after having tea and conversation with her every afternoon.

My newspaper pals put in a good word for me where possible and my dream was realized. I was hired as one of 12 guides from the state of New Jersey. I hated the thought of leaving my position as a reporter; I loved that job so much that I could not believe they paid me. However, I willingly traded all this for the incredible opportunity I had found. My friends in the newsroom all cheered when I learned that I had been hired and would leave for Europe the following March.

My newspaper pals gave me a grand sendoff at a popular restaurant in Short Hills, N.J. owned by one of the most well known gangsters in the state. We partied and dined in a lavish private room completely paid for by the gangster, who was doing a favor for our labor reporter. We celebrated far into the night, enjoying free drinks to an extent that only newspaper people could handle.

As the farewell speeches concluded, they presented me with a large drawing by the newspaper's political cartoonist. The entire staff autographed it for me. It shows me waving goodbye from a ship as a handsome man flexing his muscles welcomes me onto the approaching land. The name on the side of the ship is "Andrea Doria," an ocean liner that famously sank two years earlier after a collision, taking 52 people down with it. I framed this artwork and it still hangs on my wall, cheering me up as I fold laundry and work my way through the dreaded chore of ironing.

This newspaper job that I loved so much saved me from a difficult time in my life. Several years earlier, I had left my studies at Smith College when my father became terminally ill and we were no longer able to afford the tuition. My parents moved to California to seek medical treatment and I found myself with no means of support and no place to live. My sister and her husband offered me a room in their home until I was able to find my way.

The first job I secured was that of a receptionist/telephone operator for a local medical clinic. I hated every minute of being there and worst of all, resented that I had to work on Christmas, Thanksgiving and other holidays. Since I was low man on the totem pole, they gave me all the worst shifts.

One day my sister's father-in-law and I were discussing my situation and he encouraged me to look for a new job. He suggested that since I had always liked to write I should apply to a local newspaper. Life was easier for young people seeking jobs in those days. The requirements were not so stringent and employers were willing to take a chance on eager young hopefuls.

Although it seemed like a low percentage chance, I followed his advice, applied, and went to work for the *Morristown Daily Record*. My first assignment was that of the "inquiring photographer." I started a weekly column in which I made up a question, asked it of people on the street and took their picture with a Polaroid camera. The camera sparked everyone's interest as it was new on the market and no one had ever seen pictures develop in a matter of seconds. I drew crowds of onlookers who were amazed at the process! I had found the career of my dreams!

I remained at that newspaper for more than a year and then I was hired away by the *Newark Evening News*, recognized as one of the finest papers in the country at that time. I took the train from Morristown to Newark each morning and marveled at the fact that they were paying me. I was having so much fun at that job that I had to pinch myself to be sure I was not dreaming. Everything about it was great. I loved the sharpness of my coworkers, the challenge as well as the opportunity to be a part of such a fine organization. Most of all I was excited to be on top of the news that has always interested me. An added bonus was that this new job was a big career advancement for me. At the end of each week, they paid me in cash, the smaller amounts in two-dollar bills. I have seldom seen a two-dollar bill since.

When the ship pulled beside the dock at Le Havre, my attention was jarred back to the present and I realized that my life was changing drastically. I was far away from home and everything was going to be different. I was making a huge transition that was scary, but at the same time I was eagerly anticipating my new life with the boundless enthusiasm that only youth can provide.

CHAPTER FOUR
Brussels World's Fair
April 4, 1958

After seven long days at sea we were all thrilled to disembark onto dry land and travel by train to Brussels. My first view of the narrow gauge railroad was magical. I felt like I was a living part of all the foreign movies I had ever seen. I was finally in Europe and it appeared just as I had imagined in my dreams. The train left a glass covered station after passengers boarded their individual sections of each car - so unlike the trains in the U.S. where I had walked through rows of seats many times to find available space.

As we rode through the countryside we passed homes with backyards and pastures that all appeared to be much smaller than those in our own vast country. Flowers and vegetables were beginning to fill the space of every garden. It was spring and I could feel the enthusiasm the residents had for the new growing season.

We arrived in Brussels and took a bus to our living quarters, a newly constructed apartment building across the street from Expo 58 and a 20-minute drive from the famous "Grand Place" or Central Square of the city. Our home for the next six months would be this residence, which looked out on the famous Atomium, a huge replica of an atom and the symbol of "Expo 58"– the official title of that exposition. They assigned rooms and roommates and scheduled us for final uniform fittings. My roommate was a girl from New Jersey whom I had not known before. She was from Merchantville, N.J., a town in the southern part of the state. I saw very little of her during our six-month stay because our working schedules never coincided.

At the first fitting for our gray uniform suits, we were shocked. The pleated skirt designed by David Chrystal was just knee-length. We wore our skirts mid-calf in those days, so we felt rather risqué exposing more leg. The short-cropped jacket displayed an emblem of the United States on the left pocket and the name of my state on the left sleeve. It still hangs in the back of my closet, a treasure I have never been willing to give up.

Our shoes were the popular Capezios such as those worn by Audrey Hepburn in her movies. These fashionable low-heeled designs accommodated long, narrow feet and caused me endless pain as mine were short and wide. I spent all six months trying different sizes in a hopeless search for comfort that I never found.

A jaunty gold satin beret topped off the outfit along with white gloves, a necessary part of a lady's wardrobe in 1958.

The manager of our apartment complex was ready to tear his hair out from the beginning because he could not understand why those American girls took showers every day!

Our large bedroom window looked out on the Atomium.

That beautiful site remained brightly lit all night. The structure represented a huge atom 335 feet tall – about a third the height of the Eiffel Tower. It was the main pavilion and the icon of this World's Fair. It housed a fancy restaurant in the top sphere, which boasted of a gourmet dining experience while viewing the entire Expo Park. Reservations were at a premium during the entire duration of the Fair. The iconic structure symbolized the democratic will to maintain peace among all the nations, faith in progress, both technical and scientific, and an optimistic vision of a modern, super-technological world providing a better life for mankind. It contained eight large silver colored spheres connected by tubular arms and represented a large iron crystal enlarged 165 billion times.

Some days we would ride to work on the overhead tram that traveled on cable throughout the park. We exited at the American pavilion, a spectacular round building designed by Edward Stone (who also designed Radio City Music Hall, the Kennedy Center and many other notable buildings). This innovative structure connected to a smaller round building that housed the administrative offices by way of a long passageway.

One of my fondest memories was of walking along the passageway between the two buildings one day when the door opened at one end and a line of "Globetrotters" came toward me in their bright red, white, and blue uniforms, bouncing basketballs. These gentle giants, who were famous for their amazing and entertaining exhibitions, held basketballs in their hands as I would hold a tennis ball. They were an awesome sight in such close quarters. The Harlem Globetrotters were by far the tallest men I had ever seen and had a very friendly, cheerful demeanor.

The U.S. exhibition managers rotated our duty stations every few weeks. One of my first assignments was the IBM exhibit featuring a computer – a brand new concept at that time. We greeted guests from all over the world, many of whom were local residents. The Walloons lived in the southern part of Belgium and were the more sophisticated, French speaking people. To the north were the Flemish people, many of whom were farmers who spoke their own language.

My job was to ask the date of the visitors' birth, key the information into the computer and give them a punched card describing the important events that had occurred on that day. One of those visitors, dangling a large cigar in his mouth only inches from my face asked, "How does it know?"

One of my favorite duties was that of VIP guide. I had the honor of escorting Princess Margaret Rose of England through our pavilion. She was a lovely, small woman with the most beautiful skin I had ever seen. Another thrill came when I escorted Walt Disney, a thoroughly captivating man whose many talents have entertained the world for so many generations. He was very personable as he followed my lead and chatted along the way in a friendly and unassuming manner.

I recently found a photograph in my collection of treasures that shows me leading King Leopold of Belgium through the exhibit with a very grumpy look on my face that I believe was due to my intense concentration. This assignment was a huge honor: I considered it quite a feather in my cap that they chose me for the job. In a letter to my mother, I said how proud I was to have successfully conducted the entire tour speaking French.

During that summer, the famous pianist Van Cliburn performed in our American theatre on his way home after winning a prestigious music award in Russia. I went into that theatre many times to watch rehearsals; it was one of the many perks of the job. One day I walked in to find my idol, Harry Belafonte, on stage. I chatted with his wife and baby who were sitting next to me. I was totally enthralled by his music and remain a fan to this day.

I was experiencing thrills I never anticipated in my wildest dreams. Each day was sure to present a new one. I came face to face with Grace Kelly and Prince Rainier during their visit.

Spotting celebrities was one of our favorite games. In my letters, I said that I was very tired but was having more fun than I could ever have imagined…I was living a fairy tale life. There were so many exciting things to do that I could not waste my time sleeping. My enthusiasm and energy were boundless.

I loved working on the exhibit "Circarama," an innovative film presentation that premiered at the Fair. This was one of the most popular attractions in the U.S. exhibit. The small theater held 350 people at each showing and at least twice that many packed along the outside rail awaiting admission. They showed the film in a circular building where everyone stood the entire time. The picture was projected on a series of large screens surrounding the audience.

The attendees oohed and aahed as they went on an aerial journey that began in New York Harbor, flew across our vast country and ended by swooping down over the Golden Gate Bridge into San Francisco. The viewers had a dizzying experience while they looked down at golden wheat crops blowing in the breeze and swerved to see Hoover Dam after flying low over the rugged Rocky Mountains.

As "America the Beautiful" played in the background at the conclusion of each show my eyes filled with tears, partially from pride and partially from homesickness. This venue required that a registered nurse be on duty at all times because visitors often fainted as the wild plane trip dipped, turned, and soared over the spectacular marvels of our country.

My adventures at the Fair became more fun every day. I met young people from all around the world and greeted many friends from the U.S. who came to visit. I became good friends with a guide from the Moroccan pavilion named Johara, a beautiful and exotic young woman who shared her lifestyle, hopes and dreams with me. She later married a man who worked for the Voice of America, a radio broadcasting company that disseminated information about America throughout the world. I eventually had the thrill of introducing them to my friends when Johara and her husband came to the U.S.

I not only rubbed elbows with celebrities from the world of entertainment, kings and other heads of state but I met people who would shape our future world. We spotted famous people in the pavilion every day. I met Adlai Stevenson and Senator Estes Kefauver from Tennessee who wrote a letter of introduction for me which helped me in my later travels. I guided an Arabian Prince who invited me to join him on a trip to Switzerland.

I was unable to accept his offer as I had already made plans to leave the next day with an Air Force jet pilot stationed in Germany who had made extensive plans for our travels to Switzerland that included a water skiing adventure. Half a decade later as I went through items in my trunk I discovered a letter which that pilot had written expressing how anxious he was for me to join him in Strasbourg. In his letter he described an accident that occurred when he landed his plane in a rainstorm. He said he was approaching the runway when a thunderstorm hit. He did not have enough fuel to go elsewhere and so he came around again in an attempt to land with help from the radar "boys."

"They lost me in the heavy rain so I missed the field. I tried once again for another go at it and this time I had to land or bail out. I was coming in at the wrong angle and barely saw the runway, so when I deployed my plane's drag parachute the wind caught it and whipped me sideways. I shot off the runway at about 120 mph into a field, just missed a flock of sheep and skidded to a stop in the mud. Boy was I ever glad to get out of that bird."

Life was truly exciting in those days.

I travelled through most of Europe on my days off over that six-month period. We would often be on duty for a week or 10 days and then have several days off in a row, making it possible to travel to distant countries. I took trips to all of neighboring Europe as well as Denmark. A young man whom I had dated for four years before leaving home came to visit me in Brussels on his way back from a round-the-world trip. In fact, he left me his green cocoon-shaped sleeping bag that I later used for my own globe-circling journey. He, a friend, and I drove to Copenhagen, which I found to be one of the most charming cities I had ever visited.

When I went through the other pavilions at the Fair, I was fascinated by each new area, savoring the inviting aromas spilling from their restaurants and the interesting new sounds of their music. I wanted to see these faraway places and experience them for myself. The pavilions offered a tantalizing sampling of their cultures and customs. The restaurant in the Moroccan pavilion was a unique experience as I sat cross-legged on Persian rugs and tasted exotic foods. Turkey offered its rich coffee in small glass cups as I sat on large pillows drinking in the sights and sounds of that Middle Eastern land. When I met other guides and established fast friendships, I found that I was better able to understand their opinions as well as their criticisms of our politics…which were always forthcoming.

I wrote several newspaper articles during those hectic days and produced several feature stories for the *Newark News* that they eagerly published. They hired local photographers whose work enhanced my stories. The income from these stories helped to boost my meager finances. My contract with the US government paid only $1,000 for the six-month period of employment plus an expense allotment of $5.00 per day that totaled another $1,000. These funds did not go far, so I ate many omelets that were the cheapest thing on the menu and traveled in the most economical way possible, sometimes even by bicycle.

CHAPTER FIVE

Preparation

There was a collegial air to the guides' village at the Fair; it was abuzz with energy and tales of everyone's adventures. Through the grapevine, I heard that four girls (U.S. guides) were planning to travel around the world on their return home. This plan fascinated me because I had always dreamed of going to exotic places such as Rangoon, Burma and parts of the Far East. I became close friends with these girls and listened to their plans with great enthusiasm.

The four were Gloria from New Jersey, my home state; Sue from Owosso, Michigan; Jane from Cortland, N.Y.; and one other girl I never met. One day they told me that the fourth girl had dropped out. I had done my best to rise to the top of their "waiting list" just in case something like this happened. The remaining three invited me to join them and I was thrilled beyond words. I signed on immediately. Not one of the four of us had any money other than the salaries we were earning at the Fair, so our plan was to travel as cheaply as possible. We were able to apply the cost of our return passage across the Atlantic to our ultimate crossing of the Pacific from Asia. This was a huge windfall for our meager travel budget. None one of us was the least bit hesitant to take on this daunting adventure. As I look back, I am aware that we were a rather unique group: very few young women would have risked making that journey in 1958. We each had special expertise that we contributed to the adventure. I became responsible for the care and maintenance of the car we were about to purchase while Gloria was our stalwart document expert. Having travelled more extensively than the rest of us, she was able to handle passports, visas and any documents related to car and travel. Jane was in charge of food and Sue contributed her expertise in matters of the itinerary, drawing on the experience she had gained from living and working in Paris as an au pair to a French family.

We each had a special reason for wanting to make this trip: Jane wanted to join her family who were living in Indonesia. Sue was anxious to meet up with her friend Adnan, an attorney in Damascus, Syria, whom she had met while attending the University of Michigan. Gloria was an inveterate traveler and, like me, was anxious to see more of the world.

As I look back, I think we must have had an amazing amount of determination and courage to have taken on this journey. Even though it was unheard of for four young women to travel through some of the countries on our itinerary, we never considered avoiding those places. We just made sure that our plans were solid and our research was complete. In some cases, we would even wire ahead to the next U.S. Embassy on our itinerary to make sure that they were aware of our plans in case something untoward happened.

We spent our off-duty hours in Brussels mapping out our route and going out of our way to meet people who were living in the many countries we intended to visit. In most cases these folks would ask us to stay in their homes along the way.

We planned carefully so that we would reach Basra, Iraq in time
to board the ship that would transport our car and us across the
Persian Gulf to Pakistan and India. It was crucial that we arrive
on this date because we had already booked passage in advance
and could not change our plans unless we wanted to lose our
deposit, which, of course we could not afford. As it turned out
Iraq was the only country that we never entered and one of the
most difficult and ongoing problems we would face. We carefully
planned our route so that we could stay with our new friends
along the way and thus stretch our money as far as possible.

Two months before the end of the Fair (October 15, 1958),
we started to prepare by getting immunizations against yellow
fever, diphtheria and tetanus as well as procuring medicine to
protect us from malaria.

With our budget in mind we found a cheap clinic. We
learned the French name for each inoculation and lined up
single file in the charity ward of a hospital. Cases of everything
from abscesses to an apparent case of leprosy were treated as
we waited. As syringes were being repaired we overheard the
doctor mention *"dos"* (back) to his assistant. "I know this isn't
necessary," Sue whispered, "they don't have to give the injection
in your spine." "I'm leaving," I replied, "you know all Army
men get shots in the arm; they don't have to give them in
the back."

The syringes were prepared and there was nothing for us
to do but remove our sweaters and accept a shot in the back
of the neck. The crunching of the needles and the swishing
of the serum going in seemed worth it when compared to any
of the aforementioned diseases. On our next visit we were
scheduled for cholera shots. *Poitrine* (chest) was mentioned
in place of *dos*. "Something is wrong, that means chest and I
know that isn't necessary," I said. The other three assumed a
look of grim determination and number one stepped forward.
We each got two injections, one in each side of the chest as we
breathed a sigh of relief that we had completed our series of

shots. We applied for visas to India, Syria, Pakistan, Jordan and
Iraq as required.

Then something quite unplanned happened to me. I was
working at the Fair one day when I met Max, a handsome young
man from Switzerland. We fell in love. Max was visiting his
family and came to the Expo before returning to the Canary
Islands where he had established an import-export business.

We were immediately attracted to each other both physically
and intellectually. We had many dates and thoroughly enjoyed
our long philosophical conversations as well as the sharing of
our hopes and dreams for the future. Max was tall and slender
and spoke Switzerdeutsch – French, German, and English. Our
feelings progressed at lightning speed. Max asked me to marry
him and move to the Canary Islands. Although this sounded very
romantic and the Canary Islands would certainly be an idyllic place
to live, I had a funny feeling in my gut. I just was not quite sure I
could do it. I decided to go on the planned trip, meet Max's family
in Switzerland and see how I felt at the end of the trip. He gave
me an engagement ring and pleaded with me to join him in the
Canary Islands before I returned home.

Before I met Max, I had become friends and taken trips
with many worldly and exciting young men whom I met at the
Fair. It sounds peculiar looking back, but in those days, it was
all very innocent. I traveled with these young men to various
places in Europe and we both understood that we would stay
in separate rooms. Each of these young men conducted himself as a gentleman. The moral and sexual standards were very
different in those days.

I met another interesting young man by the name of Ken
McDonald from Virginia who had graduated from Yale with
a good friend of mine. He was serving in the Marine Corps
in Germany. He and I traveled to London and visited Christ
Hospital, a school that he had attended in northern England.
He took me to Oxford where he planned to pursue graduate
studies after his release from the Marines. We both had

wonderful experiences: he shared the places he so fondly
remembered and I was thrilled to have a guide who knew and
loved the area. Once again, there was never any question about
the need for two rooms in every situation. Life was good in
those days, I believe. Relationships were far less complicated.
While I was away for more than a year, I wrote at least fifty
letters to my mother and sister in an effort to share my experiences with them as much as I want to share it with Sophie
today. The letters were many pages long, sometimes written by
hand and sometimes typewritten. I wrote with a ballpoint pen
on the old-fashioned tissue-thin airmail paper, using both sides
because I was intent on saving postage. I sometimes wrote
on my portable Smith-Corona typewriter that I used also to
write stories for the newspaper. I finally had to abandon the
typewriter when we left Beirut and no longer traveled by car
because of limited luggage space.

As I reread those letters I find some very funny and some
very poignant passages that have surprised me and made me
realize that I am still very much the person today as I was many
years ago.

In my salad days in the newspaper business, I purchased a
green 1957 Chevy convertible which I considered the cats'
pajamas and became my most prized possession. I was quick
to point out that I had purchased it with my own earnings.
When I sailed for Europe, I left the car with my mother in
New Jersey and carefully cautioned her to see to it that my
sister and her husband did not use it to "pull out stumps." I
was well aware of their many home improvement projects and
could imagine them using my prize for this purpose.

I had dated a young man from West Orange named Charlie
who wrote to me frequently to find out when I would be available for him to visit me in Brussels. I left his letters unanswered
and in one letter to my mother I said, "Charlie continues to be
my worst problem because he keeps writing me and wanting
to visit. I just do not know what to say as he is the last person

I want to see." He continued to visit my mother weekly on the pretense of being sure she was taking care of my car. I said, "If he asks you for my hand in marriage tell him they have both been amputated. Discourage him whenever possible."

I started a letter to my mother by saying "I hope you are sitting down as this will be a shock," and went on to describe how we four girls were planning to return by traveling around the world. I outlined the careful preparations which we were making including telegraphing ahead to U.S. embassies to be sure that they would be aware if we did not show up on time in some of the more dangerous places. I described in detail the plans we were making for inoculations, emergency supplies, automobile spare parts, and told her about the friends we had made in many countries who had invited us to stay in their homes.

I described how we were fully aware of the apparent dangers but still determined to see the journey through. I added that if it would be too upsetting to her I would forgo this chance of a lifetime. She very kindly replied that she had complete trust in my judgment and encouraged me to pursue my dream with her blessing.

CHAPTER SIX

Finding the Car

As our travel plans solidified, we began to search for a vehicle that would safely take us around the world. We had our eyes on a Jeep but decided that a used American sedan would serve us better. We investigated sales by visiting all the garages in Brussels and followed up on used car ads in the newspaper.

We had decided to buy one vehicle when the owner sold it out from under us. We thought we had made all the arrangements for the purchase and it was a done deal when we learned that it was not ours after all. We were learning the intricacies of transacting business in Belgium.

I learned that a 1953 Chevrolet sedan was for sale by the public information officer at the American Embassy. The car was in excellent condition, so we made this our first choice even though the cost was $700 (more than the other ones we had seen). We understood that we could avoid the 13% Belgian tax because the car had been purchased by a diplomat in Portugal. We hoped to save some money and relieve some of the worries of our tight budget.

We later found that we could not avoid the tax as we thought, but we discovered a very involved process whereby we could bypass the payment. First, we applied to the Ministry of Finance for a tax exemption. Our next step involved a visit to the customs officer where we worked our way through the complicated and unfamiliar processes of travel documentation in Belgium.

We then drove the car across the border with the information officer's CD (diplomat) plates and carried his carnet de passage. The carnet is a customs document that identifies a driver's motor vehicle and is required in a number of countries around the world. We were able to avoid the tax by crossing the border and while in no man's land (between Belgium and France), we changed the CD or diplomatic plates for transit plates and reentered Belgium. I wrote in my journal that the customs officers had alerted the border officials that we were coming so I assume it was all on the up and up.

Gloria was the one who took charge in leading us through this complicated procedure with great efficiency as always. She had emigrated to the U.S. from Munich as a small child and had returned to her native country many times speaking German fluently. Fortunately, she had become very capable in conducting business transactions in Europe.

Gloria bought a small car when she arrived in Brussels. During our time at the Fair, Gloria and I traveled to many neighboring European countries in her tiny Deux Chevaux (a two horse powered auto).

We planned to leave Brussels at the close of the Fair but were delayed until our passports came back from Bonn, Germany where they had been sent to secure Jordanian visas. The authorities in Bonn would not issue our visas until we provided notarized affidavits certifying that we were not of the Jewish faith. The authorities would not permit travel from an Arab country to Israel or vice versa.

This delay constrained our schedule and made our timing even more critical. In keeping with our latest revised plan, we were hoping to receive our passports on a Friday so that we could apply for transit plates on Saturday morning and the *carnet de passage* on Monday. If this all worked we could leave Belgium the next day.

Miraculously all these pieces came together at the last minute and we were able to meet our schedule. We had been holding our excitement in check, but now that we had things settled, we were bursting with enthusiasm to begin our journey.

As I review our lists today, I find that the detail in our preparation was quite remarkable. We itemized our necessities and yet were careful to keep them to a minimum. I purchased a large canvas suitcase for $16 at the Army PX (to which we had access as government employees). We limited ourselves to just one piece of luggage and one sleeping bag each. We hoped that the sleeping bags would protect us from bedbugs, germs or other hazards we might encounter in cheap overnight accommodations.

While at the PX, I purchased a Minox B camera. This small item measured only about three and one half inches long and was a German product. The camera was especially well suited to my needs because it fit in a shirt pocket and I was often able to use it when people did not know that I was taking their picture. Many of these photos are used in this book.

I wore a kilt most of the time in the colder climates, thinking that a skirt would be less objectionable than pants. The kilt became useful in a way I had not anticipated: Our new friends fed us so well along the way that it became ever expandable along with my waist. The grey uniform skirt also proved very useful because it was lightweight and comfortable in the warmer climates.

We each prepared lists of items we would need for our own area of responsibility. My automotive list included 21 items ranging from spare tires and skid chains to a spring leaf (I still have no idea what exactly it is or how it functions). Other lists included medical supplies, food, extra gas and a variety of game supplies to help keep us occupied during our long drives.

The cost of the car and insurance was $806.26. Our passage on the ship from Basra, Iraq to Karachi, Pakistan had been booked in Antwerp, Belgium. We each paid $100 for this reservation and we would be required to pay another $50 upon arrival in Basra. This fee covered passage across the Persian Gulf for the four of us as well as our car.

We obtained car insurance through a Belgian company that extended our coverage through Europe, Turkey and Greece. It would expire at midnight on December 1, so we had to be sure we left Greece by that time. Payne & Co. of London insured the remainder of the journey except for our visit to Syria where we were not insurable due to the impending threat of war.

Above: The cartoon that my pals at the newspaper gave me when I left

Left: On board the USS America with fellow New Jersey guides: left to right: Judy Frankel, me, Janey Smith and Carleton Dallery. Behind them: Eleanor Levin & Monique Abbinga

pp. 35 *Above: With serious demeanor, I lead King Leopold of Brussels and his entourage through the pavilion*

Below: Me, Governor Meyner of New Jersey and fellow guides Judy Frankel & Carleton Dallery

Fair New Jerseyans at World's

New Jersey guides at the U.S. pavilion in Brussels are, from left: Gloria Teal, Short Hills; Larry Martin, East Paterson; Carleton Dallery, Montclair; Dana Matthaei, Morristown; Judy Frankel, East Orange, and Ann Garfield, also of Short Hills.

By DANA MATTHAEI

"HAVE you seen my little boy?" "I've seen about 200,000 so far today, but what was he wearing?" is the cheerful reply of one of the 215 guides at the American pavilion of the Brussels World's Fair. Then he begins to set wheels in motion for the lost child search, one of the more ordinary phases of a day's work.

Loud speakers begin to blare out messages to little Johnny throughout the pavilion in whatever language he speaks, and other members of the staff set out to look for a youngster in a red jacket.

Mama suddenly realizes he removed the red jacket and the search continues for a green sweater.

Finally Johnny is located (there hasn't been a casualty yet) and is whisked back to the central information desk in time to put through a call for Mama, who has frantically hurried off on her own hunt.

THE guide returns to his or her post and prepares for the next round of duties termed "general helpfulness in answering questions and directing the public." These duties, despite a two-week training course in language, art, politics and State Department methods of answering the U.S. critic abroad, are not to be taken for granted.

Among the staff are 15 young New Jerseyans who find themselves called upon daily to opine on anything from propaganda to popcorn throughout the pavilion. Included are the Misses Anne Carberry of Jersey City, Ann Garfield

(Continued on Page 6)

Feature article I wrote which was published in the Sunday supplement of the **Newark Evening News**

Caption reads: New Jersey guides at the U.S. pavilion in Brussels are, from left, Gloria Teal, Short Hills; Larry Martin, East Peterson; Carleton Dallery, Montclair; Dana Matthaei, Morristown; Judy Frankel, East Orange; and Ann Garfield also of Short Hills.

Fair

Eleanor Levin of Bayonne and Miss Frankel strike pose (left) at Atomium, World's Fair symbol. Above, Miss Teal's station is often in pavilion's painting gallery. Miss Matthaei, below, points to the familiar exterior of U.S. building. Of the 165 American guides, 15 are from this state.

Caption reads: Eleanor Levin of Bayonne and Miss Frankel strike pose (left) at Atonium, World's Fair symbol. Above, Miss Teal's station is often in pavilion's painting gallery. Miss Matthaei, below, points to the familiar exterior of the U.S. building. Of the 165 guides, 15 are from this state.

*Johara, my friend who was a guide
with the Moroccan Pavilion.*

*Gloria (right) and I reviewing map in my
room in Brussels with Atomium in background*

CHAPTER SEVEN
The Trip Begins
October 21, 1958

We finally received our passports and most of the necessary visas, except for the Iraqi one, which would become an ongoing problem. Our preparations were complete; we were free to begin our journey.

My three traveling companions departed together, but I had an important side trip to make first, fulfilling a promise I had made to Max. I left Brussels on October 21 and traveled by train to Zurich, Switzerland to meet him and his family.

We stayed at their home in the beautiful hills surrounding the city where I was graciously and warmly entertained.

We spoke only French the entire time since his family did not speak English. Max and I later drove from Zurich to Rome in his black Citroen sedan where I would meet up with the other three girls.

The drive to Rome was beautiful. Max and I traveled through the dramatic, snow covered Alps to the St. Gotthard Pass. They loaded our car onto a flatbed train. We sat in the car for a long time as the train passed through a pitch-black tunnel. When we reached the end of that blackness, the bright light revealed a beautiful land, lush with warm sunshine, palm trees and tropical plants. We were entering the Canton of Ticino, the Italian speaking, southernmost area of Switzerland. We had a beautiful leisurely lunch on a terrace overlooking a lake and later saw the school that Max had attended.

I spent two wonderful weeks in Rome with Max, his sister Eliane, her husband and their child. They showed me every significant sight in that beautiful ancient city and its environs. We shopped for food daily in the many little neighborhood markets, buying meat in one place, produce in another, making an adventure of the outing. This was a charming alternative to our trips to the super market at home where we typically stock up for the week and try to get the shopping done as fast as possible. Max and I sipped coffee in small outdoor cafes and frequented all the places that most tourists do not even know about.

We took day trips to Napoli, Amalfi, and Sorrento. We saw the famous Mt. Vesuvius in the province of Naples well known for the eruption that destroyed Pompeii in 79 AD. I remember visiting a museum where I saw the remains of a man lying in the fetal position who had died instantly from the volcanic gases.

Just before leaving Rome, a friend gave my hosts tickets to the celebration of the upcoming Papal election. We were in Vatican square when the white smoke rose from the chimney signaling that they had elected Pope Pius XXIII.

After our wonderful stay in this famous city, Max left to return to the Canary Islands. I felt horribly sad at our parting. We had grown to know each other well and shared so many wonderful times. We talked enthusiastically about a future together...but I was still not convinced that I would marry him.

He encouraged me to go to the Canary Islands before returning home, but I knew that I could not disappoint my family. It was a very bittersweet moment when we parted; along with my sadness, I was setting out on the adventure of a lifetime.

At last the much anticipated day was here – we were beginning our round the world journey! We four had only met six months earlier when we arrived in Brussels but were confident that we had what it took to make it through the next few months of challenging travel.

Gloria appeared to be the most mature of our group. She was self-assured, unflappable and almost matronly compared to the rest of us. She was tall, dark haired and always wore colored nail polish. Gloria seemed to be the most reliable, dependable and understanding friend each of us could find.

Sue always had a broad smile on her face and was eager to go along with any plan we made. She had dark hair also and was of medium height. Sue had always had a problem with her weight and proudly told us that she had lost 30 pounds while she was in Paris working as an au pair. She explained that she had done so by not eating dinner in the evening. Sue had a lovely singing voice and was always eager to cheer us up with a happy tune. She was wonderful at keeping our group on an even keel.

Jane was perhaps the least mature of the group and always needed to have it her way. She was the eldest of three children, perhaps the reason why she felt she always knew best. Jane was always ready for an adventure. She was never afraid to take the first bold step into new territory and therefore helped the rest of us feel confident. Her eagerness to reach Indonesia and reunite with her much loved family kept us going through some very tough times.

I was (and still am) the smallest of the group and was well aware that I was lucky to be a part of the cadre. I was an add-on and wanted to prove my worth. I was very anxious to visit the exotic places listed on our itinerary and had no doubt that I could handle any difficulty. After all, I had managed to get this

far and I saw no reason why I could not make it all the way.
Gloria and I became the closest of friends during the trip,
probably because we had similar personalities and always faced
each situation with maturity and determination. We had fun
but when it came down to brass tacks, we were the ones who
would get the job done.

I recently contacted Sue and explained that I was having
difficulty describing myself for this book, so she gave me a
short description: My fellow travelers looked upon me as
capable and businesslike. Sue found me friendly and outgoing
because I had made many more friends at the Fair than she
had made. Not surprisingly, she described me as small and
very athletic.

We four girls met up and began our round the world odyssey
by driving our 1953 Chevy to Florence. When we arrived, we
checked into the first of a long series of youth hostels that
would provide us with beds on which to place our sleeping
bags and cold water for morning showers. The sleeping bags
were a necessity as we were determined to avoid any vermin
that might be lurking in bedding material.

The cost was 35 cents a night for lodging and 45 cents for
a big meal at student rates, including wine. Sometimes we
purchased food that we cooked and ate in the hostel using the
camping equipment we brought along to save money.

My most memorable sight in Florence was the sculpture
of "David" by Michelangelo. I found this treasure completely
awesome in its remarkable detail. We saw all the tourist attractions by day and went to bed exhausted at night, having walked
everywhere to save money.

Because of the journal I kept, I am able to recount the
details of our travels 56 years later. I noted that although the
youth hostel group was not my preferred crowd, the conditions
were not unbearable. Cold showers were surprisingly easy to
take when I considered the cheap price and the length of the
journey that was ahead.

I added, "I think I can maintain my dignity no matter where I find myself. The important thing is cleanliness and this I can see to." I guess I was an old lady even at that young age. I went on to say, "I am anxious to get going on the trip. I need to read more books and study more about all parts of the world, but I feel quite confident that I will do so."

We travelled from Florence to Venice where I marveled at St. Mark's Square filled with pigeons. We were excited to find that we were required to park our car in a lot outside the city and then travel only by water taxi or gondola.

We left Venice at 10:30 one morning and arrived in Innsbruck, Austria at seven that evening where we found a youth hostel in the basement of a school. This hostel had heat and warm water, luxuries that made us feel like we were in a first rate hotel. We ate a delicious full meal for 35 cents and loved the comfort of a warm shower.

Continuing through Salzburg and Kitzbuhl, we drove to Vienna and spent five days visiting their many tourist attractions, including the Spanish Riding School and the beautiful Schonbrunn Palace.

We checked on our visas at the Iraqi Embassy and learned that they had no information for us. We had applied for the visas on September 9 in Brussels and it was now mid-November. Each time we made an inquiry they told us to wait. This happened in Brussels, Rome, and now in Vienna.

I noted in my journal that the recent "outbreaks" in Iraq might prevent us from entering the country but we planned to try once again when we reached Istanbul, Turkey.

CHAPTER EIGHT
Yugoslavia
November 18, 1958

We left Vienna on November 18 and drove to Graz,
Yugoslavia where we bought bread and cheese for a cheap
picnic lunch along the roadside. We began to travel through
a territory that was foreign to us. Europe had been an
adventure, but most of the customs and mores had been
somewhat familiar.

We were now entering a completely different part of the
world and countries that had vastly different cultures. The
challenge was to find our way and survive. We were all very
worried deep down, but did our best to be brave for each other.
For the most part, we tried to be as cheerful as possible and
did not express our personal doubts and misgivings.

The roads were in a poor state of repair and almost im-
passable in some places. As we approached the border, things
started to get very strange. They were guarding the border

station much more tightly than others through which we had passed. When we entered Yugoslavia, our first non-European border crossing, it was daunting. They required us to declare all of our belongings such as typewriters, cameras, etc. We had not been required to do this at other borders.

They allowed us to carry in only 3,000 dinar each, in denominations no larger than 100 dinar notes. (We had exchanged our dollars for Yugoslav money in Brussels thinking that we would get a better rate, but it turned out that we were wrong. We had received 550 dinars per dollar and found that we could get 700 per dollar in Yugoslavia.)

Therefore, we found ourselves with far more Yugoslavian money than was permitted. Gloria and I went into the ladies' room at the border station and stuffed our bras with all of our large bills to hide the fact that we were "accidentally" defying the rules.

Next, I learned that my visa was not acceptable; when it was issued in Brussels an error had been made. It had been validated through November 18, the day of our arrival, instead of December 18. After waiting an hour, they allowed us to continue, but told us to go to the U.S. Embassy immediately upon arrival in the next town to have it changed.

Crossing the border, I noticed that there were huge differences in landscape, architecture and lifestyle. We left Europe and were now unmistakably heading toward the Middle East. There were very few cars on the road and only a few scattered houses. I was having a "strange feeling" akin to the feeling I had when visiting East Berlin, where rundown buildings had been covered with false facades. We noticed that the store windows were very plain, displaying only a few utilitarian clothing items.

Maribor, the first city we entered, was then a part of Yugoslavia, but is now in Slovenia. Their language at the time of our visit was Serbo-Croatian. After economic and political crises in the 1980s and the rise of nationalism, Yugoslavia broke up into smaller countries consistent with their ethnic origins. Today the independent countries of Slovenia, Croatia, Bosnia and Herzegovina, Macedonia, Serbia and Montenegro have all emerged from within the post-World War II boundaries of Yugoslavia.

We were apprehensive and a little afraid as we entered this new country. None of us spoke the language; although we had made it a point to learn the basic polite questions and replies. We had a hard time following road maps and signs written in the Cyrillic alphabet, which we found confounding. Here is an example of "Independence Road" translated into Cyrillic: Индепенденсе Роад. Imagine that on a map or road sign! We located a tourist agency and asked where we could find rooms. There were no youth hostels so the young woman at the desk gave us the name of a cheap hotel and told us that two women would show us the way. We were relieved to find that at least one person in this town could understand and speak English.

Gloria and I walked out of the agency and spotted the women talking to a man in the street. The man walked ahead of our car to lead us and, much to our surprise, he also spoke English and was able to interpret.

The desk clerk suggested that we bring our car into a small courtyard to keep it safe. Jane tried to negotiate the narrow passageway but was unable to maneuver since our American car was so much larger than those the road was built to accommodate. I got behind the wheel and was able to drive through the narrow space while a crowd of about 60 local people gathered to watch and cheer me on. This was our introduction to the many crowd scenes we would draw along the way; we had not realized what a phenomenon four young American women travelers would become.

Our self-appointed interpreter said that he would return after we settled in. When he reappeared, we found him to be a delightful person whose name was Ivan. He joined us for dinner, bought wine and coffee for us and invited us to visit a wine cellar the next day. He turned out to be a teacher in a local commercial school. Ivan spoke perfect English and saw to it that we learned everything about his hometown. We were relieved and encouraged to find that we could make our way in this completely unfamiliar area and that we were able to communicate without knowing the language.

This was our first clue that people throughout the world were welcoming and friendly. At the end of the trip, I remarked that people treated us with kindness and hospitality throughout the world. Although it was very unusual for four young girls to be travelling alone in these remote places, no one ever tried to take advantage of us nor did we ever have a bad human experience. The world was a kinder and gentler place in those days.

CHAPTER NINE
Zagreb, Yugoslavia
November 19, 1958

The next morning we ate bread and jam in our room in
Maribor before setting out to meet our new friend Ivan. He
escorted us to the embassy where we secured an extension for
my visa.

Ivan took us to a local museum that featured the horrors
of World War II. The exhibit described the Nazi invasion and
brutal occupation as well as the destruction caused by wartime
bombing. He explained that his country was grateful to the
Americans for liberating their country, although U.S. bombs
had caused much of the destruction.

We set out for Zagreb after lunch and found the roads to be
in good repair although we seldom passed a car along the way.
The area through which we drove was scenic and rural. We

traveled up and down lush green rounded hillsides that looked like someone had groomed them with an electric razor. The people we passed appeared to be farmers as they walked along the road or traveled in horse carts.

We reached Zagreb after driving 110 miles and made our usual stop at a hotel in search of rooms. The clerk spoke very little English but indicated that the hotel was full. However, he put us in touch with a young man who was able to help. He told us that he had also been a guide at the World's Fair and spoke perfect English.

When we returned to our car, we found two other young men waiting, one of whom was very handsome (he resembled Marlon Brando). They offered to help us find rooms in private homes; they said it would be less expensive than a hotel. They led us to our quarters, made all the necessary arrangements and even carried our bags upstairs. We all went into town where we ate sandwiches and learned that "Marlon" was a student at the university who lived in Split and wanted to become a film writer.

The next morning the two young men arrived when we were eating a simple breakfast while "Madam" or the woman of the house boiled water for instant coffee that we had brought with us. "Marlon" and his friend took us to their home where we were treated to Slivovitz – a distilled beverage made from plums – frequently called plum brandy. Gloria, in her quiet but humorous way suggested that we describe this episode in our journals as "eat, drink and be merry" or "around the world in a bottle."

Our friend who had been a fellow guide took us to two different wineries where we tasted delicious Dalmatian wines and then bid him farewell. He described his sadness in seeing us go and was almost to the point of tears. I imagine that his stay in Brussels had been the highlight of his life and that our visit had brought back many happy memories.

CHAPTER TEN
Belgrade, Yugoslavia
November 21, 1958

Our next stop was Belgrade, a city that had grown rapidly and was the capital of the renewed Yugoslavia as well as a major industrial center. We drove along a major highway for 393 kilometers or about 250 miles from Zagreb. An excellent road took us through wide plains in windy, cold weather assuring us that winter was coming. We amused ourselves on the long drives, playing games and attempting to learn a few more words in Serbo-Croatian. Sue led us in a few songs and Jane insisted that we stop and have snacks along the way.

We pulled into a roadside station for petrol and met a young man named Don Somerville from Oregon who was traveling in the area. He offered to wait for us outside the city so that he could guide us to the Putnick Hotel, an accommodation he suggested where we could secure rooms for 550 dinar a night. When we entered this metropolis (about 6,000 people), we noticed that they were building many new apartment complexes and industrial buildings. The city seemed to be not only expanding but also thriving economically.

Don treated us to drinks and dinner at a very nice restaurant where we heard Gypsy music, reminding me of my visits to the Hungarian pavilion at the World's Fair. Don pointed out Yugoslavian Prime Minister Josip Tito's son, who was sitting at the bar and was very drunk. Apparently, Tito had disowned him so he became a colonel in the Russian army.

Don took us on a tour of the city the next day beginning with a visit to a Russian Orthodox church. The building was strikingly different from any other church I had ever seen. It was a large rectangular building with onion shaped domes topped by gold plated crosses. The interior had three main parts, the vestibule, the temple proper and the altar or sanctuary. The major difference in these buildings is that there are no pews or seats in the main area. A few seats were provided for invalids, but in former times only those that could afford to pay were seated. The regular parishioners stood during the entire service. A large, imposing building stood on the other side of the street and was the home of the archbishop.

We went to an outdoor museum high on a hill overlooking the convergence of the Danube and Sava Rivers. We viewed the spectacular sight from high above on the grounds of an ancient Belgrade fortress. Heavily forested riverbanks lined the edge of the deep flowing waters.

The museum featured exhibits and relics of both world wars. Yugoslavia was divided in World War I: the regions of Slovenia, Croatia, and Bosnia fought on the side of the Central Powers (Austria-Hungary and Germany); while Serbia and Montenegro fought on the side of the Allies. During World War II the area was overrun by Nazi troops, but a persistent guerilla force fought relentlessly.

The weather was misty and cold, about 35 degrees Fahrenheit. We felt the biting cold and dampness growing every day, an uncomfortable situation since we had not packed many warm clothes.

We left Belgrade early the next morning and continued south for a 14-hour drive to Skopje over the poorest road conditions we had travelled so far. The surface was so bad that we could only go about 25 mph. The constant jostling broke off our tailpipe. We only passed about 10 cars during the full day's ride.

The brightest part of the journey was when we passed a wedding party in horse carts who insisted that we share their celebratory drink, a strange warm liquid that tasted, let's just say, odd. The party rode along in 10 richly decorated carts that they had festooned with colorful flowers; even the horses had flowers in their halters. The bride wore a long white veil and white dress covered by a tattered old black coat, a necessary addition in that cold, damp climate.

Other people we saw had strong Mongolian features and rode in carts drawn by skinny old horses, oxen or even cows. The countryside was barren and flat until we neared Skopje and climbed into high hills. We took a wrong turn and went almost 25 miles out of our way, a frightening experience since it was dark by that time and there were no road signs to guide our way.

When we reached Skopje (which is now the capital of Macedonia), I was bitterly cold, dirty from road dust and car repairs and hoping for a hot shower – which of course, was not available.

We left at seven the next morning for Greece along difficult, rough roads where we passed only crude huts and a few scattered monasteries whose architecture was decidedly mosque-like.

CHAPTER ELEVEN

The Accident
November 25, 1958

Salonika was the first city we reached after crossing the border from Yugoslavia into Greece. We started late the next morning because we waited for some Turkish travelers we had met in Skopje who were going to Istanbul via by the same route we had chosen. They offered to show us the way and we gladly accepted. Any help was a blessing as far as we were concerned. We had our first blowout and were glad the Turks were there to help change the tire.

We were doing our best to negotiate a very windy pass, but lost our way because of our inability to read the road signs. We strayed 75 kilometers out of our way and almost crossed the border into Bulgaria. Unfortunately we had lost sight of our Turkish pals and had to muddle our way through deserted back roads until we got back on track.

We finally rejoined them at a hotel in Lamia, Greece where they introduced us to a drink called Raki, strong liquor that tasted like licorice and would turn milky when mixed with water. The drink was by no means our favorite, but it was soothing and relaxing as we finally started to feel safe after a long hard day.

The next leg of the journey from Lamia to Athens began at about 5 a.m. We drove over roads that were even more difficult and had to stop several times to let herds of sheep cross in front of us. Sheepherders would always wave to us in a friendly fashion and hold up one hand in a thankful gesture while we waited sometimes for 45 minutes to let the entire herd clear the road. Apparently no one rushed things in this part of the world.

About 42 kilometers from Athens, we reached a steep mountain pass. We began to ascend the precarious terrain, navigating the narrow road and hairpin curves as slowly and cautiously as possible. That was only half the battle! We were carefully maneuvering the downgrade on the wet, slippery road when our wheels locked and we slowly started to skid toward a large oncoming truck loaded with produce. We were out of control and terrified! The brakes were having no effect on the icy surface…we could not avoid crashing.

Thankfully, we were able to stay on the road, since the drop off on the side was straight down a rocky ledge. The slow grinding impact completely smashed our left front fender. Our damaged radiator pushed into the engine block, knocking it off kilter.

Thank heaven no one was hurt, but we all felt a little sick from the narrow escape. We wondered how we would deal with this situation, our first real emergency. Gloria and I assessed the damage while Jane fretted that we would never be able to drive the car again. Miraculously, within a matter of minutes a group of men in a truck stopped and offered to help.

The passenger door of the truck opened and a police officer who was hitching a ride stepped out. More trucks, buses and cars stopped behind us. No one could get through, which heightened the state of confusion. Since none of us spoke Greek and the gathered crowd spoke no English, French or German, we attempted to communicate by sign language. They helped us move the car to the side of the road so that traffic could pass.

CHAPTER TWELVE
The Aftermath in Athens
November 28, 1958

Jane and I decided that the best solution would be for us to take a bus to a nearby village in order to find a tow truck. We hesitated to board the vehicle but knew that we needed help and this seemed to be the only way to find it. We hated to leave Gloria and Sue standing in the road but consoled ourselves in knowing that at least there was safety in numbers, and none of us was alone.

We had only travelled for five minutes when the other passengers began to wave their hands frantically in gestures that we took to mean that we should get off and take another bus in the opposite direction. We looked at each other, confused and worried, but left the bus to do as the group seemed to be suggesting. Soon a second bus came along from the other direction and we boarded in hopes that we were doing the right thing.

The new bus was just as smelly and crowded as the first had been. As we passed right through a small town, we became even more nervous. The bus stopped along a barren stretch of the road to pick up a man who was holding a strange looking telephone. He seemed to be gesturing to us that we should use it, but since this was long before the days of cell phones we had no idea what he meant. We never did figure out why he was carrying a phone, but were too involved in our own problems to worry about it.

The bus driver finally let us out in Thebes where we followed the man with the telephone to a café/restaurant where, by some miracle, they spoke English. I remarked to Jane that this was the filthiest place I had ever seen: cans and garbage were strewn all over the place.

We were explaining our plight when a middle-aged man with unruly black hair and a full beard stepped forward and introduced himself as John Saffo. He welcomed us and said that we could secure a tow truck next door. Apparently the word had travelled far and fast that four young American girls had been involved in an auto accident.

John served us a cup of coffee and sent a boy next door for the truck. The boy soon returned to report that the driver was out of town but would return sometime that day. We were not sure what we should do but decided that we had no other option so we would wait no matter how long it took.

Our new friends were able to find another driver…but he did not have a license…so we waited and waited some more. We worried about Gloria and Sue stranded out there on the road. The time passed like an eternity. Meanwhile more and more local folks began to arrive to see the American girls. We waited for hours drinking strong black coffee while people poured in to get a glimpse of us. They had friendly smiles on their faces but had no qualms about looking us over from head to toe at close range.

John Saffo was wonderful to us. He explained that he had a cousin living in Dover, N.J. and that he had lived in Portland, Oregon for 13 years. I could not help but wonder why anyone would return to this godforsaken spot after living in Portland.

After many long hours, the locals found a driver and tow truck that took us back to the scene of the accident. The huge vehicle moved at a snail's pace over the narrow road while the fog slowly began to creep in and thicken.

Our driver was not able to use headlights in the fog, so we stopped when each vehicle approached, pulled over and let it pass. Jane and I were terrified as we navigated the hairpin turns and looked down hundreds of feet into the precipices below. We worried that we would not be able to find our friends and the scene of the accident, especially in this fog. In fact, there were not many roads in the area and everyone seemed to know just what and where it had happened.

When we reached our car both Don and Sue were waiting and told us that Gloria had gone on into Athens to report the accident to the embassy. Don had come along after we left for help and was able to give moral support if nothing else. They loaded our car onto the truck and we girls rode with Don in his car into the city of Athens. It would be difficult to describe the immense relief we all felt when we finally arrived.

When we met up with Gloria, we learned that she had handled her responsibility well in her usual fashion and had completed the accident report. We were very lucky that there were no injuries because if there had been the driver would have faced a jail sentence. Greek law decrees that the driver is always at fault and in the case of injury the guilty party would go to jail.

We reached Athens at about ten o'clock that evening after signing more papers and went straight to the garage where our car was stored. We realized that our ordeal was not over. We scrambled to find a phrase book so that we could communicate. By no means were we feeling confident.

When we reached the hotel that Gloria had found we all four collapsed into our beds completely exhausted.

The next day we returned to the garage and arranged to have the car repaired at a cost of $150.00. We decided to take a ship from Piraeus across the Aegean Sea to Istanbul. The fare was $88 for our car and the four of us. At that point we just had to hope that the car would be finished by the time the boat sailed in four days. We did not say the words aloud, but none of us was very confident.

The following day we enjoyed Thanksgiving dinner at Don's apartment; he was living and working in Athens at that time. After dinner he and I visited the Acropolis by moonlight. I remarked that the building was a beautiful pure white by night but was a yellowish pink by day. The heavy smog of Athens had taken its toll. We were three days behind our scheduled departure from Athens due to car repairs, but we made good use of the time by visiting the many important tourist sites.

One day we drove to Marathon with Don and walked the site of the legendary battle in which the brave Athenians, though greatly outnumbered, defeated the invading Persian army in 490 BC. Then we drove on to the Temple of Poseidon that sits atop a high cliff overlooking the beautiful blue Aegean Sea. It was one of the loveliest panoramas I have ever seen.

In my journal, I noted that the people of Athens had been wonderful to us. *"Each individual we meet is kinder and more generous than the last."* I continued, *"And I can very well see why the Greeks were so inspired in their cultural pursuits: they have such magnificent natural surroundings."*

CHAPTER THIRTEEN
Istanbul, Turkey
December 2, 1958

It was our good fortune that the Greek mechanics proved to be very competent. Our car was ready on time and seemed to run well. And so on December 2 we drove from Athens to the port of Piraeus to embark on the next leg of our journey.

They loaded our car onto the deck of the "Ege," a large cargo ship that would carry us across the Aegean Sea to Turkey over a period of 36 hours. We watched as they chained the vehicle to a crane and slowly lifted it on deck. They then lashed it to stanchions with heavy chains while we stood by wondering why they needed so many heavy chains to secure it. We felt very protective of our automobile and watched every step of the way making sure that they did not damage it in any way.

We found our accommodations, a dormitory in the bow of the ship, which we would share with about 20 women.

The Turkish and Greek women sharing our cabin were dressed in black shrouds. Only a few of them had any teeth. They were all in their bunks by one in the afternoon, shortly after we left port.

We soon realized why the heavy chains were necessary when the wind began to whip up and the swells grew bigger. We were heading into a storm! We all remembered very well our recent Atlantic crossing and feared for our future. It soon became a night of horror! When we first hit the full force of the storm, the rocking of the boat was kind of fun for me because I enjoyed the gentle rocking motion and have never been seasick. But when the rolling and pitching started to intensify, our fellow passengers began to vomit all over the cabin. I realized in horror that my canvas suitcase was on the floor floating around in all kinds of nasty debris. Finally Jane and I could no longer stand the miserable stench and loud chorus of moans so we went up on deck and spent the rest of the night in our car.

The sea was rough, even worse than our Atlantic crossing. We hit one big wave after another without any respite and I wondered if the ship could survive such a beating. Then I began to worry that the car would break loose from its chains and be propelled into the sea. We lived through the night, but I still do not know how.

The next morning the ship made a stop in Izmir for a few hours so we disembarked and enjoyed the fresh air and solid footing. Nothing could have been more welcoming than that solid land; it had only been one overnight but it felt like an eternity.

I had not seen a toilet seat in about a month and the bathroom facilities on the boat made those in any railroad station back home in the U.S. look like heaven. We boarded the "Ege" once again for the short trip to Istanbul. Jane and I raced back into the hold to grab our suitcases and run, holding our noses all the way.

Approaching the beautiful skyline of Istanbul, outlined by mosques and minarets, we realized that we were now entering a very different part of the world from any we had ever seen. The legendary city was known as Constantinople in ancient times and was (and still is) one of the largest cities in the world. Istanbul straddles the Bosporus Strait, one of the world's busiest waterways, between the Sea of Marmara and the Black Sea. The commercial and historical center of Istanbul lies in Europe on one side of the strait while a third of the population lives on the other side, in Asia.

We made our way down the gangplank and our friend Sadat Ergun stood smiling at the bottom to greet us. We had met him at the Fair where he was serving as head of security for the Turkish pavilion. Sadat held an even more important job in the capital city of Ankara as head of the criminal department of the police force for all of Turkey. He had travelled to Istanbul to meet and guide us through his country as he had promised in Brussels.

He shook three fingers at us and explained that he was very upset and worried while waiting for us for the last three days. Sadat kept reminding us of this by holding up the three fingers and repeating "three days" in Turkish. Naturally, he expected us to arrive as scheduled, but was very concerned when we did not show up. He had been checking the border crossings for three days expecting us to arrive by car. He finally came to meet this boat on the chance that he would find us.

Unfortunately, communications were not as sophisticated as they are today and we could not let him know that we would arrive late because of car repairs. We felt terrible that he had been so worried and expressed our appreciation for his being so considerate.

We immediately took our car to a nearby garage to have the wheels aligned and later followed Sadat to our hotel. He explained that the arrangements we had made to stay with the parents of a guide from the Turkish pavilion were "inconvenient," so he told us that they all agreed that it was best for us to stay in a hotel. He very kindly insisted that he pay for our lodging, for which we were very grateful.

We visited the famous Blue Mosque, a beautiful structure that accommodates 10,000 people for prayer. We gazed in awe at the vast interior, which was empty on the morning of our visit. Turkish rugs covered the floor; upon entering, we were required to put paper covers over our shoes. The very high ceiling is covered with mosaic painting in a rich blue color while the lower part of the walls are decorated with blue and white tiles.

We learned that the men always face Mecca (east) when praying and that they pray three to four times daily. Only men can answer the call to prayer in this public place. A strange sounding voice comes from atop the minaret calling the men to prayer. First they must wash thoroughly – hands, face, neck, ears, arms, head and feet – and then they bow down in a prostrate position in neat rows giving their responses in unison. The acoustics in the mosque are so perfect that if one leaves a watch on one side of the building he can hear it ticking on the opposite side.

Sadat drove us through the city and out to the Bosporus where we enjoyed tea and hubbly bubbly, the process of taking in smoke through a long tube filtering it through water. This was just tobacco smoke, not marijuana, for which they used water pipes in later years. (I attribute much of the success of our journey to the fact that drug trafficking was virtually un-heard of in those days and did not present any threat to us.)

We returned to the hotel, called the parents of our friend the Turkish guide, and learned that they had, in fact, expected us and were waiting for us to join them for dinner. We never figured out how this misunderstanding occurred but we moved out of the hotel and into their home the following day.

Sadat completely filled our day with plans. He took us to the police station and on to an outdoor market where people were screaming to hawk their wares, most of which looked to be of very poor quality. Completely skinned animals hung from hooks, still dripping blood. The produce looked like it had come straight from the field, without any cleaning or refrigeration. The cooked food was very spicy, mostly lamb dishes and pastries that were exposed to flies and other insects hovering above – a most uninviting sight to us.

He drove us to the Iraqi Embassy where we learned that they had received a letter from Brussels regarding our Iraqi visa application, but had not yet received a reply from Baghdad. We forwarded a telegram to Baghdad in hopes that we would get a reply when we arrived in Damascus, Syria, our next port of call.

The earliest that we could expect a reply would be in two weeks and by that time we would be in Damascus and would have to decide which route we would follow for the rest of the trip. The Iraqis were threatening to have a revolution and therefore the area was becoming more dangerous every day. The people at the embassy looked askance at our plans as they pointed out that people were already evacuating the country. We realized that we might have to sell our car in Beirut and fig-ure out a completely new way of getting to Pakistan and India.

Sadat hosted a fancy lunch at a beautiful restaurant along the Bosporus where they served some kind of brains for the first course and fish complete with head and tail for the second course. Both Jane and I covered up the ends of the fish as best we could and swallowed hard. We continued to push the food around on the plate to make it look like we had eaten.

After lunch, Sadat introduced us to the chief of police who drove us to Topkaoi Palace. We had special permission to visit the 104-year-old edifice that was not open to the public. It housed beautiful Bohemian crystal including a chandelier that hung elegantly in the ballroom and weighed 600 pounds. We saw the room where Ataturk, the first president of Turkey, died in 1938 as well as the harem section, separated from the rest of the palace by three iron doors. The elaborate marble bathroom had gold fixtures and priceless marble accoutrements that represented two thirds of the cost of the whole palace.

While we were working at the Fair we went out of our way to meet people from the countries through which we planned to travel. We did this partly because it would be less expensive but mostly because we felt that it would be the best way to learn about the local people and their ways. Sadat was one of our "finds." He was certainly very, very kind and showed us more of this city than any other tourist would ever see.

Just before we left Istanbul to visit Sadat's home in Ankara, we had breakfast at the home of another friend whom we had met at the Fair. Her name was Gugene. We felt very sorry for her because she was only 19 years old, but looked to be 25. Even worse, Muslim tradition would not allow her to leave her house alone or have any kind of a job or career.

Gugene had spent the summer in Brussels where she was free to go wherever she wished and now she found her life very frustrating. More than anything, she wanted to go to the United States. It was difficult for us to comprehend her situation, as we were all four independent young women who had completely taken charge of our own lives. We regretted that we were not able to help her and felt sad that her chance of getting to the U.S. was very slim.

CHAPTER FOURTEEN
Ankara, Turkey
December 9, 1958

Our drive from Istanbul to Ankara took about eight and one half hours. It was an easy trip for once. We drove over paved roads all the way, except for when we climbed Bolu Mountain, where we navigated muddy ruts in a howling wind. Fortunately it did not start snowing until we came down from the mountain and rejoined paved roads on level ground.

Sadat's wife and family greeted us in a very warm and friendly manner when we arrived at their home that afternoon. I was surprised to find that his wife looked about 10 years older than her age of 27. Women aged very quickly in that part of the world.

Sadat was the only family member who spoke English, so we struggled to communicate with the others by sign language. His grandmother lived in the home and loved to sit by my side when I wrote letters on my portable typewriter. Each time I paused she made hand signals for me to continue. She was a sweet woman, seemingly quite old, with hardly any teeth. As soon as I resumed my typing, she began to snore.

After sleeping in real beds for the first time since Rome, we got up at a leisurely hour and followed Sadat to a museum featuring an historical assortment of Turkish police uniforms. We saw the uniforms of the early officers who wore a turban, a belt that sheathed a scimitar and baggy balloon pants. Their uniforms changed from the days of the fez style hats to the current 1958 styles in which they wear britches, hats with visors and navy blue jackets with metal buttons. Sadat very, very proudly showed us this exhibit.

The next morning we went to the offices of the U.S.I.S. (United States Information Service) to investigate if it was possible to obtain Iraqi visas. Mr. Wells, the public information officer, took us into his office and updated us on the volatile Iraqi situation. He explained that a revolution was brewing and that there was virtually no law and order in the country. He went on to tell us that if Iraqis spotted an American car they would steal it because they are so poor. They would not hesitate to kill the occupants to prevent identification. He suggested that we take alternate routes through eastern Turkey and Esfahan.

We tried to find out if there was a way to go from Beirut by ship but there were no agents in Ankara so we decided to wait until we arrived in Damascus. We agreed that we most certainly would have to cancel our booking from Basrah.

We spent many wonderful days with Sadat's family. Their hospitality was outstanding but their standard of living surprised us. Sadat had an important job and earned an above average salary, but the family's basic lifestyle seemed low. They still used a potbellied wood stove for heating and cooking.

The next day I visited a dam with Jane and Turquar, a young man who we found very interesting. He had spent six years in the U.S. studying engineering at the University of Michigan and spoke English. He was eager to share information with us about his country. Turquar explained that Turkey was in very bad shape economically because the party in power had messed up two years earlier by spending money out of the country and not making provisions for the future. Therefore, it was illegal for them to have foreign currency and it was just about impossible to leave the country except as a student.

He went on to explain that although they had a democratic system, there were no selfless or honest leaders. He seemed to think that the socialist party would have been a better choice and he hoped that they would win the next election. He told us that 80% of the populace were peasants and were uneducated.

One of our most exciting adventures came about when I met up with the other girls in a Turkish bath in Ankara. The building was in the worst slum section of downtown. The place was scary enough, but the clientele who were entering were even scarier. We hesitantly followed our friend Sabina inside as she paid the fee and ushered us upstairs through a blast of steam and a puddle of water two inches deep.

She led us to a small cubicle that contained two wooden benches and some hooks for clothes. Sabina sat right down and began to strip. We all looked at each other and modestly began to remove a few items of clothes, slowly. When we reached the point where we had taken off the bra and slip, we all decided that that was enough.

We wrapped ourselves in towels, put on wooden slippers and followed Sabina downstairs like four scared rabbits. We passed several old hags along the way who were naked to the waist and were wearing baggy diaper-style pants. Passing through a steamy room that led into a large marble lined bath, we suddenly entered what seemed like a Reubens painting. Huge fat women were completely nude exposing their large hanging breasts. We looked at each other and Gloria said, "I don't know about you, but I will not be taking off my underpants!"

Sabina threw a few buckets of water on us and the fun began. Each woman stared at us as intently as we stared at her. They had shaved their bodies and walked around holding their private parts. They soaped themselves all over, including their heads.

Sue lay on a marble slab while one of the old crones with breasts hanging down to her waist started to rub her all over. She turned Sue over and gave her the same treatment on the front, which produced wads of dead, black skin. She had bathed the day before and could not figure out why the black scum came off her body.

The rest of the clientele threw a few pots of water on themselves, shaved, and proceeded to rub off their calluses with pumice. Meanwhile all the dirty water, excess skin, etc. was draining straight out to the street – adding to the other debris in the open sewers. We returned to our locker area and quickly dressed. Our underpants that we had refused to remove were so wet that we had to take them off. We left in a hurry, still trying to figure out the mystery of the black skin.

We returned to Sadat's house where his sister dressed us in local costumes and took our picture. We retired to our beds early, because not only were we exhausted from the bath caper but we also knew that we had to be up very early the next morning to continue our journey.

CHAPTER FIFTEEN
Adana, Turkey
December 13, 1958

The drive south from Ankara to Adana introduced us to a completely new and exotic part of the world. As we left Ankara, we came to our first desert and were surprised to find that it was not sandy as you might expect but a barren wasteland covered with brown dirt.

We spotted our first camel caravan and turned to each other with big smiles on our faces, thrilled. Jane and I almost jumped out of the car; we were both animal lovers and had not expected to see these exotic creatures along the way. The string of camels was loping along the side of the road with that funny undulating motion that no other creature seems to employ. Rough, coarse looking people were leading the caravan and appeared threatening but surprised us with smiles and friendly waves. We stopped to take their pictures and decided that the land had an almost biblical look – unchanged from 2,000 years ago.

We continued through rugged, wild looking country and were pleasantly surprised to find well-paved roads. About 80 kilometers outside of Adana, our car blew another tire. When the car swerved back and forth, we felt the telltale thumping and knew that we were in for trouble. We jacked up the car and changed the tire, but our momentary satisfaction in our ability to survive was shattered when the jack became stuck and would not release.

Each of us tried, repeatedly to make it work, but the jack remained firmly stuck under the car. We scoured the horizon, but no one was in sight. A feeling of hopelessness settled upon us like a thick fog.

But the fog lifted soon enough, thankfully! As our friend Sadat said, "Good Chance" was following us. A truck came into view, stopped, and four men jumped out to help. They reached into the back of their truck and gave us some oranges and grapefruit to eat while they released the jammed jack.

We made our way to the next petrol station where 15 men joined in to repair our tire immediately. They used our vulcanizing equipment, because they did not have any of their own. We were pleased to find that our extensive preparation had paid off!

Another small truck came along with a well-dressed Turkish man inside who chatted with us as his driver inflated our tire. He explained that he was on his way to Adana and insisted that he follow us in case there was any further trouble along the way.

When we arrived in Adana our new friend found us a hotel room, sent up tea and located a garage in which he parked our car overnight for safekeeping. He told us that he was a sales representative for the largest soap company in Turkey. He appeared to be middle aged, was of medium stature, had a full head of dark hair and a well-trimmed beard. He had just learned the concept of advertising and told us how excited he was about passing out free bars of Puro soap as he drove through the main streets, touting his wares over a loud speaker.

Our soap salesman insisted upon meeting us at six the next morning to make sure that we got a safe start. He was amazed at our courage because he said he would not even drive from town to town in this area with his wife. He did explain, however, that the Turks liked to help foreigners, especially Americans. Once again, we were amazed at the hospitality that these people were showing us.

Upon reflection, I realize that this was just the beginning of a journey in which people treated us with kindness and generosity all around the world. It was unusual to see four young American girls in those faraway places, but no one ever tried to take advantage of us in any way. Thinking back it seems astonishing, but the world is simply a far different place today. The vast improvement in communication has made the people of the world far more sophisticated but also much less trusting of their fellow man. I know now that we were very lucky to have made our travels when we did.

I wrote in my journal on Dec. 15, 1958:

"This was the most fantastic day so far!"

We left Adana at 6:30 a.m. after our friend the Puro soap man paid our hotel bill, gave us cookies and candies and led us all the way past Iskenderun on our way to Syria. The road was excellent when we crossed over the Nur Mountains to Iskenderun on the east coast of the Mediterranean Sea. We continued southward toward Syria and noticed that the people were getting rougher looking. In fact, they seemed ferocious to us. We all squirmed with uneasiness. They lived in crude mud/grass huts and were coarsely dressed, but fortunately did not prove menacing at all. Everyone greeted us with a smile and a friendly wave as we passed by.

We arrived at Turkish customs at 11 a.m. where they served us tea and did not bother to check any of our documents. We entered a four-mile "no man's land" and agreed that this was something that no man would wish to claim. Craggy rocks and barren hills were all we could see, it looked like nothing could

or would grow here. We passed the ruins of two crusaders'
castles, one of which they called "the Castle of the Girls."
They named the entrance to the place "Love's Door," which
we theorized must have described a well-equipped inn for the
ancient travelers.

When we reached the Syrian border the gates were locked.
We had no idea what we would do next when a border guard
unlocked the door and ushered us inside. We were thrilled to
find Sue's friend Adnan waiting and Sue was ecstatic because
this was the reunion she had long awaited and her reason for
making the trip in the first place. She had not seen Adnan
since he was in Michigan studying law. Adnan facilitated our
entry by telling the officials that I was a newspaper reporter,
which seemed to bear a great deal of prestige. They did not
even check our luggage. We later learned that the USIS had
taken our picture in front of Ataturk's mausoleum in Ankara
and many newspapers had published it; therefore, we were
quasi-celebrities and were welcomed as such.

As soon as we entered Syria the landscape changed
drastically. The soil was red and very fertile looking, particularly
well suited to grow their major crop of tobacco. We passed
many Bedouins, men in long white robes wearing turbans on
their heads.

Another tire blew shortly after we crossed the border. The
weather was miserable, freezing cold and rain was pouring
down, but we had no choice other than to face the elements
and change the tire. When we got the new tire in place, we
discovered that once again the jack was jammed. We flagged
down a car for help and six Arab men rushed to our rescue.

The ordeal lasted over two hours while we shivered and
groaned in the wet and cold. Finally, we were able to continue
on to the next town for repairs. We patiently sat in the shop
drinking coffee and trying to learn a little Arabic – we always
tried to learn a little of the language of our next country so
that we could at least say, "hello, please, thank you," etc.

When we got back on the road one hour later we had another flat. This time we knew we were in a very dangerous area because military forces surrounded us. Thankfully the jack released after we finished changing the tire. We finally reached the next town at 1 a.m. and could not find a repair place open…so all five of us slept in the car until a shop opened early the next morning. We were glad that Adnan had joined us; we felt better protected with a man on board.

CHAPTER SIXTEEN

Damascus, Syria

December 15, 1958

We spent more than three weeks in Damascus and enjoyed an extremely busy social life filled with parties, fancy dinners and sporting events. We got the shock of our lives when one member of our group announced that she would not be continuing the trip with us.

The United Arab Republic, bringing Syria and Egypt together, was established in February of 1958 but it turned out to be short-lived. In 1961 Syria seceded from the union. At first the Syrians were very much in favor of this alliance because it provided security against potential aggression from Israel. However many Syrians soon realized that there were considerable disadvantages. They felt that Syrian standards were higher than those of the Egyptians. Syria boasted a rate of 60% educated citizens. Egyptians, on average, were far less educated.

The Syrians were very concerned that Egyptians would move to their country and lower their standards.

Before long Egyptians were flocking to Damascus, selling photos of their President Gamal Abdel Nasser, door to door. Syrians felt obliged to buy these photos and display them in their homes or workplaces because Nassar was the head of the UAR at that time.

When I received letters from home I learned that they were censoring our mail. I tried to convey to my mother that I was very uneasy about the tenuous Iraqi situation without saying it in so many words. It was becoming more and more evident each day that Iraq would not permit us to enter and therefore we would have to change our plans.

Adnan arranged a meeting with the Saudi Arabian consulate in hopes that we could obtain visas and continue our journey via his country. If we followed this route we would have to go by ship through the Suez Canal, south through the Red Sea, and cross the Arabian Sea north to Karachi. All that would add considerable time to our trip. We investigated every port from which we could depart for Pakistan.

When we arrived at the consulate for the meeting Adnan had arranged, a dark skinned man wearing a turban and an outfit that looked like a nightgown greeted us. He ushered us into a large office with floors covered in plush Persian carpet. The gold trimmed Louis IV furniture that filled the room fascinated me. It was almost blinding in its opulence.

The Saudi Arabian consul was a neatly goateed, immaculately dressed man in his early thirties sitting behind a huge desk at the far end of the spacious office. Behind him was a large bay window providing a view of the entire city. The consul was handsomely dressed in the latest western attire. He told us that he had attended Cornell University and received his PhD from Harvard. His father had been the king's personal physician and because he died while in service, the government appointed his sons to important positions.

The consul explained that it would be impossible to issue Saudi Arabian visas because women could not travel or even appear in public unescorted by men in his country. We all looked at each other surprised. We believed that as Americans we would not have to follow strict Islamic custom.

This meeting was disappointing, but ironically, the consul ended it by inviting us to dinner the next evening at the airport restaurant, the finest place in town.

The following day was an amazing sports day. We went out with about 10 young friends of Adnan to play tennis, ping-pong and basketball. We spent the evening at the home of Adnan's uncle where we sang, laughed and toasted everyone's good health with a spirited and friendly group of his relatives.

On Saturday evening, the Saudi Arabian consul arrived to take us to dinner in a large white Cadillac limousine. They seated us at the best table in the house right on the edge of the dance floor. The eyes of everyone in the room were riveted upon us the entire time. The other diners stared at us for long periods of time, which made us a bit uncomfortable, but we were slowly getting used to it. We drank scotch in highball glasses while the consul sipped his scotch from a teacup, refilling it frequently from a small teapot. We danced, ate, and made plans to go camel riding the next day before retiring at 2:30 a.m.

The consul invited us to join him another evening, this time for an authentic Arab meal. The large white Cadillac limo took us to an apartment where a dark skinned servant in Arab dress stepped out and greeted us.

"Is this the consul's home?" I asked.

"Of course not," came the reply. "He could not entertain you with his wife present!" Gloria whispered that she was not sure what we were getting ourselves into. I agreed, but we entered the large plush apartment anyway since it was too late to turn back at that point. We walked into the large living room and breathed a sigh of relief when we saw John Blake and his wife, an American couple whom we had met earlier. They greeted us with big smiles and as usual, the party began with lots of scotch and lively conversation.

Sultan, the cook, acted as host and announced dinner. He was a remarkably handsome and a well-built former professor of sports who lifted weights to keep in shape. Sultan spoke about four words of English but managed to let us know that he wanted to come to the U.S.

He presented the meal on a huge platter – the body of a roasted baby lamb with eyes wide open, lying atop a mound of rice and peas. The other guests all looked longingly at the eyeballs, the part they considered the greatest delicacy. We tried very hard to mask our feelings when we saw the poor little creature. I glanced over at Jane and hoped that she would not express her feelings against animal cruelty.

We ended the evening by having more drinks at the Blake's apartment, a luxurious and beautifully furnished home. They were a lively couple who stayed up drinking and partying every night until 5 a.m. and then slept until noon. They had two small children who nannies raised. We learned that John Blake was the son of an American diplomat and had been born in Tangier. Mrs. Blake was from Pennsylvania and had studied in Italy and Spain. They told us that they hated living in Damascus because they seldom met new people and the local folks never invited them into their homes. Their social life was limited to a small portion of the embassy set.

We talked until the wee hours of the morning when Mrs. Blake rose to her feet, "I guess I'll go to bed," she announced, "so I will be able to get up tomorrow at least by one or so, and do something. I don't know what yet – maybe tell the maid to remove the cobwebs."

She explained that she could not do anything productive or she would be taking the job away from a servant. She had a full time cook and housekeeper so there was very little for her

to do but drink and sleep. Her husband was an author but had
not written anything in their year in Damascus.

The following day, Christmas Eve, the Blakes invited us
back to the same apartment for pancakes, a meal that was
very soothing to our hangovers. We returned to the home of
Adnan's brother to help decorate and wrap the meager gifts we
could offer our friends. The family hosted a party that evening
for several neighbors, one of whom kept asking me to dance
with his son who was playing the accordion while his mother
sang off-key. Gloria was the only smart one in the crowd: she
excused herself to go to church. Overall, I concluded that it
was a depressing Christmas Eve.

We spent Christmas day visiting many friends who insisted
we continue to party that night. We had attended too many
parties so we made excuses and returned home to bed at 10.

We soon realized that we would never obtain visas for Iraq
and therefore had to find another way to get to Pakistan and
India. One of our options had been through Saudi Arabia, to
sail from Dammam on the east coast of the Sinai Peninsula...
but now they told us that we could not enter that country.
We considered going through Kuwait but learned that was
impossible for many of the same reasons.

Driving through Iran seemed to be a possibility, but we
knew it would be a challenge, negotiating a hazardous mountain road in wintery, snowy conditions. One other option
would be to sell the car, but we found that the duty charges
would cost more than it was worth.

Things were not looking good for continuing our journey.
There seemed to be plenty of obstacles and a severe shortage
of solutions.

As we prepared to leave Damascus, we faced the most
shocking and saddest news of our whole journey. Sue, one
of our steadfast fellow travelers, informed us that she was not
going to continue the trip with us.

Sue was in tears while she explained that she had decided to marry Adnan and remain in Damascus. She presented it as anything but joyful news and I knew something was wrong. We tried gently to get her to elaborate a little, but Sue was simply not forthcoming with any details about how she and Adnan had reached this decision.

CHAPTER SEVENTEEN
A Short Visit to Beirut, Lebanon
December 30, 1958

We drove to Beirut in search of securing an alternate route to Pakistan and India. We left on my 25th birthday, December 30, and began traveling through the barren hills of Syria that resembled all the pictures we had seen of the Middle East. The sunsets, though, were the most magnificent I had ever witnessed. They began as vivid lilacs and blended into fiery red colors in a gorgeous progression, a display that lasted much longer than those I remembered at home.

When we reached the Syrian border, we spent an hour clearing passport control and another half hour at the customs office down the street. We met a student from Tripoli, Libya who asked us for a ride. I said that he looked small and harmless, so we agreed to take him along.

We drove some 20 kilometers through no man's land and reached the Lebanese border. Since we had no Lebanese money, our student friend made an exchange for us and immediately proved his worth.

The scenery became more and more interesting as we neared Beirut. We crossed a high, forested mountain range with many upscale resorts. The bombed out buildings near the border were a reminder of the centuries of wars that have been fought in that region.

As soon as we entered Beirut, we immediately encountered a huge traffic jam. Both pedestrians and vehicles filled the streets, which were restricted to one-way traffic for cars but two ways for trams. I drove along cautiously, never knowing when I might meet a tram coming straight at me from around a blind the corner.

Tensions were very high in Beirut. Just the previous July bad feelings between Christians and Muslims had escalated so drastically that a civil war seemed imminent. The U.S. military had intervened to install a tenuous peace.

We checked in at the YWCA where we paid four Lebanese livres each (about $1.25 per night). We went out to an Alfred Hitchcock movie that evening, passing three police roadblocks in the center of town. The extra security was frightening because we were not sure whether new political unrest was brewing or if this was standard practice. Our information was limited since all news reports were in Arabic which none of us understood. People gathered around and stared at us while we ate in a sandwich shop. We were the only women to be seen anywhere.

Our sojourn in Beirut was into its second day when we connected with a travel agent who assured us that he could arrange for bookings on a ship out of Kuwait. He said that he had sent a wire to the shipping company and would have a reply in a few days. We returned to Damascus to rejoin Adnan and our new friends in time to keep our promise of attending their New Year's Eve celebration.

    Despite the turmoil, Beirut proved to be a most interesting place. Tension and security were high and the streets were teeming with people but the setting was lovely. It was a tropical paradise that reminded me of Florida with its balmy breezes and swaying palm trees, a lively resort town here along the eastern Mediterranean Sea.

CHAPTER EIGHTEEN

Political Intrigue
January 4, 1959

We returned to Damascus for a celebration hosted by our new friend Haddad whom we had met through Adnan. The New Year's Eve festivities began at 9:30 at the best restaurant in town and included hats, horns, dancing and a never-ending supply of drinks. In the wee hours of the morning we all went to the Blakes' home for dessert.

I received a phone call one morning from a man we had met named Bichato, asking me to play tennis. Gloria and I accepted and played with two German women while Bichato sat on the side and chatted with another man. Bichato's friend said that he would arrange a game for the next day.

After tennis, they took us to a mutual friend's house for tea. The "friend" turned out to be a young couple who lived in a palatial home. We became suspicious of these people and wondered why everyone seemed to be very well off but no one seemed to be going to a job each day.

We continued in this tennis/party mode for several days, playing tennis while the men sat on the sidelines and talked It all came to an abrupt halt when Adnan gave us some alarming news. He informed us that the local version of the FBI questioned him about us and our association with Bichato and his friends. He insisted that we no longer see them…and we certainly did not argue, as we knew that he was serious.

Apparently, they first spotted us at the airport restaurant. The authorities were keeping close tabs on us because one of the men who befriended us was a member of the nationalist party that had assassinated an important general. His anti-communist party was swinging too far in the other direction. The authorities believed they were plotting against the regime in power.

Adnan revealed that he had told the local security office that we would be arriving in the country, explained our situation, and they cleared us for entry even before we arrived. However, they had kept close tabs on us the whole time and had become suspicious when we associated with these men. We surmised that the men were using us as a cover for their secret political meetings.

Gloria suggested that we should be more cautious in the future, although we were in a difficult situation considering the language barrier and our unfamiliarity with local customs.

On the morning of January 4, we awoke to find that our difficulties were escalating rapidly. Our departure from Kuwait was postponed until February 14. We knew that we could not impose upon our hosts any longer and, to make matters worse, our visas would expire in a few days and they would not extend them.

We learned from Adnan that the security office had actually been following Gloria and me ever since that first night when we met the Blakes. They knew our names, knew that we had gone to Beirut, and believed that we intended to meet with the U.S. military attaché.

The officials became even more suspicious when they found that we were seeing our new tennis friends; this was the "final straw" that prompted them to summon Adnan to the office of the minister for questioning. They obviously thought that we were spies for an American agency. This was the reason why they would not extend our visas!

We analyzed the entire sequence of events and concluded the only explanation was that John Blake was so blatant in his dislike for the present regime that they were keeping close tabs on him. Therefore they did not trust our association with John and his wife.

The intrigue deepened when we received a mysterious phone call from someone named Eva who asked us to come to tea so that she could "talk to us." She told us an intriguing story.

Eva revealed that she had left Soviet-dominated Budapest, Hungary 10 years earlier by joining a dance company. This was the only way she could find to get out of Hungary. She was performing in Beirut with the dance troupe when her passport expired and she was in danger of deportation.

Eva realized that the only way she could remain in Beirut would be to marry a Syrian. She managed to find a husband and although she hated living in Damascus, it was far better than the alternative.

She told us that she had spent three months in Europe the previous summer and made no bones about the fact that she had lived in Berlin for a week with an American Army Major. Gloria and I tried not to show our shock at this revelation, but we were not accustomed to the open admission of adultery. We were having our eyes opened in so many ways that it became difficult to absorb. We felt sorry for her poor husband who seemed to be a good guy and was being taken for a ride.

Eva was apparently looking for a shoulder to cry on or possibly a way to get to the USA through our contacts. Everyone we met seemed to have an ulterior motive…and that was beginning to concern us even more. We worried that we had bitten off more than we could chew and realized that we had to leave Syria right away!

The atmosphere was grim; we learned of more and more people who hated living in Damascus. We were finally able to leave on January 11 – almost a month after we had arrived in the city – a place we had planned to visit only because of Sue's friendship with Adnan.

CHAPTER NINETEEN
How Will We Continue?
January 11, 1959

We returned to Beirut on January 11 where our friends helped us to find a nice, clean, cheap hotel, "Jerusalem House." We remained on the party circuit because many of our friends from Damascus had come to Beirut and continued to host us at fancy restaurants every night. We even enjoyed cognac at the famous Cave des Rois in the Excelsior Hotel.

One of our acquaintances arranged to have us driven to Baalbek, a historic town about 60 kilometers north of Beirut. As we traveled along the coast, we passed many large rocky cliffs with grottoes in the clear blue Mediterranean Sea. We saw snow covered mountains in the distance as we noticed poinsettia plants growing all over the hills. Banana and orange trees laden with fruit lined the side of the road. When we reached Baalbek we visited the famous ruins of the temples of

Jupiter, Venus and Bacchus. These are some of the best-pre-
served Roman ruins in all of Lebanon. They established the
town 9,000 years earlier and it has been continuously inhabited
ever since. The large stones on the temples were delicately
carved and remain intact after many centuries.

A few days later, I wrote in my journal, *"We are still in
Beirut and I don't know if we will ever find a suitable way
out."* I added, *"The only consolation is that we continue to
meet fascinating people and therefore learn a lot more about
life here each day."*

Jane and I decided to go to the port in Beirut in hopes of
finding passage from Pt. Said, Egypt to Pakistan. We entered
the office of a booking agent who told us that only two lines
operated between those ports and the fares were very expensive. I began to think the whole pursuit was hopeless when
Jane insisted that we explore one more possibility. She had
more determination than any one I have ever met. She would
not give up on any project she had started whether it be saving
a stray animal or finding a solution to a problem.

We knocked on the door of what appeared to be a shipping
company. A nice looking young Arab man offered to help
us. He was sure he could solve our problem. He introduced
himself as Mike Haddad and asked where we were staying. He
said that he lived in an apartment near our hotel and asked if
he might have a lift home. On the way home he adjusted our
engine to idle faster as it had been stalling out and invited us to
his apartment that evening for drinks. He turned out to be a
most helpful friend.

Gloria and I once again pursued the possibility of selling
the car but found that the Lebanese customs fees would be
$800 and the car was only worth $500.

Ever hopeful, Gloria and I went to the American embassy
again to try to find a buyer. As we waited in the lobby, the
Ambassador stepped out of a large black Cadillac limousine,

holding his black Poodle on a leash. His valet, dressed in traditional Arab style, rushed to hold the door for him as the dog tended to his business in a nearby bush. When the Ambassador entered the building, his valet ran to the elevator and pushed the button so that his employer would not have to wait. This struck us as excessive service but the marine guard on duty explained that the French ambassador enjoyed the same amenities. Servants were abundant in those days as most people were desperate to find work and labor was cheap.

In a final attempt to sell the car, we decided to go to Amman, Jordan where we had heard of a possible buyer. We headed back to Damascus in order to get to Jordan. When we reached the Syrian border all of the officers rushed out to greet us with open arms. We had passed through so many times they began to welcome us as friends. In fact, one of them said, "Hello Dana, the Damascus police were here asking questions about you."

Back at Jerusalem House in Beirut, we were sitting in the lobby discussing our plans one day when a tall young American man by the name of Stewart Mott walked in and struck up a conversation with us. He was dressed in bohemian clothing and wore beaded leather moccasins on his feet. He had a long ponytail and tied a woven band around his forehead. Sue recognized him immediately because he was from her home state of Michigan. In fact, his father was chairman of the board of General Motors.

When he heard of our trip to Jordan, he asked if he might go along. He had been traveling for a long time and had just returned from Afghanistan where he picked cashew nuts during the summer. He seemed like a nice guy and would be able to help pay for gas so we agreed to have him join us. We were pleased to have him along on the first leg of the journey when we experienced our ninth flat tire and he repaired the faulty jack.

Meanwhile Mike had booked passage for us on the "Steel
Vender" out of Beirut on January 22 which would take us to
Alexandria, Aqaba, and finally to Karachi, Pakistan at a cost
of $200 each over a period of 12 days.

Stewart told us that he had been to Tehran, Iran and
Afghanistan and would be able to show us the way if we
would continue our trip his way. He even offered to go with
us. This route would take us to Pakistan by land rather than
by sea. He said that his way would cost less as he could get
student rates on an airplane. This sounded much better than
spending 12 days on a freighter zigzagging our way to Karachi
so we decided to accept his offer and asked him to start
working on reservations. In the meantime, we would continue
with our trip to the Holy Land, as it was included in our basic
itinerary and would fit in with our plans to go to Amman to
sell the car.

CHAPTER TWENTY
The Holy Land
January 21, 1959

Once again, we returned to the Syrian border and headed south. As we drove into Jordan the land became more and more barren and flat – a dry, brutal desert. We passed a few Bedouins living in tents in the dunes. We travelled to Amman, the capital of Jordan, which is the country's political, cultural and commercial center and another one of the oldest continuously inhabited cities in the world.

Amman had been a small city until 1948 when the population expanded considerably due to the influx of Palestinian refugees. During the 1948 Palestine War (in Israel the war is known as the War of Independence because it established the State of Israel), some 700,000 Palestinian Arabs fled or were expelled from what is now present day Israel. A combination of force and fear motivated this mass migration.

The Palestinians fled to the West Bank and Gaza and to the contiguous countries of Syria and Jordan. The bitter feelings created by the situation explain the reason why they would not issue visas for Israel once we had been to an Arab country.

We traveled the American built road easily and to our delight the signs were in English. We approached the area near the Dead Sea, which reminded me of the Grand Canyon. The road led us down, down, down to a body of water which is fed by the Jordan River and lays 1,401 ft. below sea level – the lowest elevation on earth. We did not get out of the car but drove right on to Jerusalem as we planned to come back and visit on the return trip. Number one on our agenda was settling our automobile problem.

About three miles out of Bethlehem, we ran out of gas. Luckily, we had prepared well for any emergency, so we pulled out our jerry can and refilled the tank…only to discover that the engine still would not turn over.

A middle-aged man on a motorcycle stopped to help. He explained in English that his job was to guard the newly planted trees along the roadside. People were so poor that they would steal anything to sell for subsistence. He tried to start the car but had no luck either. A taxi driver next tried, failed, and flagged down his friend, a truck driver, who determined that there was water in the line. The truck driver, Salim, completely cleaned the filter and found that we needed a new valve for the pump. Salim and Stewart climbed into the taxi and headed for Jerusalem where they purchased a valve and worked for three hours to install it. Once again, we met people who were generous of spirit and eager to help us. Everyone who passed by offered to assist in one way or another.

Our helpful truck driver suggested that we go to Bethlehem for the night, as he knew of a cheap hotel. The taxi driver led the way and Salim took up the rear in his truck to be sure that we were safe.

We checked into the Bethlehem hotel and found it to be the dingiest accommodations we had found so far. We took the only available room, which was set up for six people. Stewart would have to be in our room. We looked into the bathroom and discovered that the toilet was just a hole in the ground. This fixture had the colorful nickname "bear prints over a bombsight" – which aptly described the platforms on either side of the hole. Luckily, we had developed a way to deal with these smelly bathroom situations by dousing a tissue or handkerchief with cheap perfume and holding it under our nose.

Salim and his friend took us on an hour's walk through the town after we had settled in, despite the fact that they had just been working for three days and three nights. It was a magical evening! I found that Bethlehem was truly the silent little town described in the Christmas song, just as I had imagined it would be all my life.

Bethlehem lay on a quiet hillside and I got the impression that it had not changed in 2,000 years. The little narrow cobblestone streets were completely silent after 8 p.m. The stars and the moon were the brightest that I have ever seen that magical night. I could well imagine that it was a night just like this when Jesus was born in this quiet little town. All the men (the only people on the street) were dressed in sheik-like outfits and covered their heads in traditional Arab scarves.

When we talked with the locals, they told us that they had no future. They pointed out that the land they now inhabited was nothing but dry unworkable soil. They sat around the streets passing their time because they had no work and nothing else to do.

We arose early the next morning to attend a church service in the Church of the Nativity where Jesus was born in what is now a small grotto.

The following day we found a tourist bureau in Jerusalem recommended by the manager of our hotel in Beirut. We hired a guide for a half day. His name was Zachariah, a tall, skinny Arab who soon became our best friend.

The old city of Jerusalem is divided into four parts: the Armenian, Muslim, Jewish and Christian quarters. It is only about one kilometer across and is a walled in city within the modern city of Jerusalem. You enter the city through a series of gates. It is only accessible by walking because of the very narrow cobblestone streets and steps.

Zach took us through the divided city, pointing out the 14 Stations of the Cross marked along the Via Dolorosa, meaning "Way of Sorrows," which is held to be the path that Jesus walked carrying his cross on the way to his crucifixion. We saw the markings on the stones that the Roman soldiers had carved while playing their games centuries ago. Zach led us to the Church of the Holy Sepulcher, the site where Jesus was buried, a small grotto in the basement of the church.

Zach led us to the site of the original water storage facility that still supplied water for the old city. I walked through those narrow passageways and felt that very little had changed in the last 2,000 years; I was sure that those small stone buildings would still be there in the next two thousand years.

We returned to Bethlehem to pick up our luggage and ran into our original taxi driver. Amazingly, he offered to buy our car for $625. We were tempted, but agreed that that was not quite enough. Then, as soon as we returned to the modern city of Jerusalem, people suddenly were in a frenzied bidding war for the car! One of Zach's friends, a prospective buyer, invited us to the one and only nightclub in town. When we stopped to pick up Zach at the barbershop along the way, a stranger came up to me and offered to pay more than anyone else had offered. Suddenly the car had increased in value and none of us had any idea why.

We returned to our hotel at about 1 a.m. Early the next morning buyers were pounding at our door. We settled the whole matter and agreed to sell the car for $725 to Jack's brother-in-law who assured us that Jack would pay up when we returned to Beirut. We were confident that this would work out and were proud of ourselves since we had only paid $700 for the car in Brussels.

CHAPTER TWENTY ONE
Jericho,
West Bank Palestinian
Territories
January 22, 1959

Our next visit was to Jericho and the Dead Sea. We found Jericho to be just as described, a true "oasis in the desert." The name Jericho means "fragrant" and it is a perfect definition of the city, which lies just north of the Dead Sea within the West Bank area of the Jordan River. The ancient city was founded in 9,600 BC and is prominent in the Hebrew Bible.

Jericho was occupied by Jordan from 1948-1967 and has been held under Israeli occupation since the Six Day War in 1967. They handed over administrative control to the Palestinian Authority in 1994.

The Hebrew Bible (Old Testament) describes the old city as "The City of Palm Trees, a true oasis." Copious springs in and

around the city have attracted human habitation for thousands
of years. It is known for being the site of the decisive Battle
of Jericho that secured the Israelites' return to the Promised
Land from bondage in Egypt. Joshua led the Israelite army
around the city blowing their trumpets. Thus, we have the
well-known hymn that keeps repeating in my head, "Joshua
Fit the Battle of Jericho."

We returned to the Dead Sea where Jane and Stewart swam
in what looked like dirty, cloudy water. In actuality, it is just
extremely salty – so salty that they could float with no effort,
much like the Great Salt Lake in Utah. We sat by the sea for a
long time chatting with our guide turned friend, Zach. He told
us sadly that he could see no future for himself in that land.
He wanted to go to the U.S. but knew that he had little chance
of doing so.

Everyone we met was more than eager to talk openly and
seemed to know as much about our American foreign policy
as we knew ourselves. They looked upon the U.S. as the place
they wanted to be, although they knew that they would never
be able to afford to leave the Middle East.

Our friends insisted that we go to the Dead Sea Hotel for
drinks. We explained that we first had to complete the bill of
sale for our car, which turned out to be a hand-written note
scribbled on a piece of paper.

We returned to Syria the next morning. Jane, Stewart and
I waited in the customs office while Gloria completed the
necessary documents. I happened to see a copy of *"Buick
Magazine"* in which I read about Stewart's father, Charles Mott.

The next morning we were up early in Beirut for our first
shower in seven days! We went to Mike's apartment to sort out
our belongings since we would no longer be travelling by car.
Meanwhile Stewart helped us secure visas and airplane tickets.

We called Jack (the new owner of our car) in order to
collect our money. He explained that he was very busy throughout that day but he planned to take us to dinner and give us

his check that evening. Conducting business in these countries was very difficult for us so we took great care to respect their methods and tried to be patient.

We went to the American Embassy where they gave us full instructions, warnings and precautions before entering Afghanistan. This was a very scary situation when we learned of the possible dangers we could face but it piqued our interest and buoyed up our adventurous spirits. Our only security was in knowing that Stewart had been there and he was sure that he could safely guide us through the country.

When we returned to our hotel, we received a phone call from Ariana Airlines, the national carrier of Afghanistan, based in Kabul. They informed us that our plane would be leaving for Tehran at 2 a.m. instead of the scheduled 8 a.m.

Since the banks would not be open at the time of our early departure, we had to find a way to cash Jack's check before we left. He called the bank president and arranged for this transaction to take place at the airport the next morning. We were exasperated and worried about the narrow margin for error. We knew that we had no choice other than to get to the airport and hope that the manager would perform as promised.

We returned to our hotel and received an updated message from Ariana Airlines letting us know that they planned to pick us up at 12:30 a.m. Then they called again to say that they were unable to send a car, which put us into a new quandary. Luckily, Jack volunteered to drive us to the airport where the plan came together, thank heaven, and we cashed his check. We then transferred the funds into traveler's checks, which was the only safe way to carry money in those days.

We breathed a huge sigh of relief as we had solved one of our biggest problems. At the same time, we were apprehensive about setting out for a new and scary country about which we knew very little.

CHAPTER TWENTY TWO
Tehran, Iran
January 21, 1959

We learned that Ariana Airlines was a subsidiary of Pan Am and felt a little reassured in heading out to this far different part of the world with them. The Middle East had become reasonably familiar and comfortable, but now we were again adventuring into new and unknown territory.

Our group of four now included Stewart instead of Sue. The plane accommodated only nine passengers, the four of us and five members of a Pan Am family: a father, mother and three small children. There were nine seats in the fuselage; the rest of the space contained cargo secured by heavy nets.

The roar of the motors and the laborious struggle down the runway made us wonder if we would ever achieve lift-off. When we finally climbed into the air, we discovered that we could see light around the edge of the door. We stuffed the edges with rags from the cargo area to reduce the noise, although the roar of the engines was still deafening.

We played bridge on our makeshift table, a briefcase where we kept all our important papers. We were able to catch catnaps for brief periods throughout the night, but we were too apprehensive to sleep for any length of time.

Looking out one of the few windows, I could see only barren land. The snow covered mountains converged into a desolate brown plain scattered with mud huts. I awakened to see Baghdad, a beautiful sight by night, with its mosques and minarets outlined by sparkling lights. We were flying over what I imagined to be a thrilling and exotic city and it evoked thoughts of a magic carpet skimming the rooftops.

The plane continued through the night, laboring at low altitude over barren flatlands. As the pink rays of the sun began to appear, the pilot swooped down several times and finally landed at the Tehran airport. It was a nine and one half hour time change from my home in New Jersey.

The airport building was modern and comfortable, though the weather outside was bitterly cold and rainy. We found a hotel that we could only describe as "ratty." All four of us shared one room. As usual, the toilet was a hole in the floor. They gave each of us a bucket of cold water for washing. I went to bed feeling sick and did not awaken until nine the next morning, feeling refreshed after a good night's sleep.

We walked around Tehran in the daylight and found it to be a bitterly cold, rainy, muddy city – the most unappealing place we had yet visited. I could not understand why anyone would want to live here, but I gave them the benefit of the doubt and conceded that we were visiting at the very worst time of year.

At four that afternoon, we met Stewart's friend Misha, a Russian Jew with whom he had become acquainted on his previous trip. This young man was dressed in typical Iranian attire and sported a long, dark beard. After he served us a welcoming cup of tea, a custom in the area, he suggested we go square dancing at the American Iran Society. The Iranians were crazy about square dancing and were thrilled to have us join them. When the dancing ended, we dined at the Grand Hotel Ferdowsi on a typical Iranian meal of lamb and rice delicately flavored with saffron, nuts, herbs and dried fruits.

The following day we obtained our Afghan visas and found a doctor who could give us the necessary inoculations to protect us in the next countries on our itinerary. They had run out of typhus serum but he said this was unnecessary and gave us a prescription for anti-plague medicine instead.

He x-rayed my knee, which had been hurting, and found a fracture: a small piece of bone had broken off my kneecap. I was sure that this had occurred when I was playing field hockey in school, but the cold, damp weather in Iran was now causing stiffness and pain. Decades later when I had knee surgery, I was given the bone fragment in a bottle, preserved in formaldehyde.

We ventured into our second Turkish bath that afternoon and thankfully, it was more upscale than its counterpart in Turkey. This place offered private cubicles, which made us much more comfortable. The experience pleased us more the second time around. We knew what to expect and were really feeling the need of a bath by this time.

Misha hosted us at the airport restaurant that evening where we danced to a live band. We continued on to another nightclub and returned to the hotel at 3 a.m. People seemed to enjoy their nightlife immensely in these countries. The days were so bleak that we began to understand their reasoning.

On Sunday morning we went to the famous Golestan Palace, the oldest historic monument in Tehran. The Qajar Dynasty built the complex of buildings when they were in power from 1794-1925. They adorned the palace with brightly colored mosaics and delicately hand painted tiles. We admired the lovely pools in the courtyard, which led into an entrance hall lined with huge Bohemian crystal mirrors. Magnificent Persian rugs softened the floors, and the throne and bed were inlaid with precious jewels. Despite the lavish details, it was the warmest palace I had ever visited and the only one in which I could imagine living.

We bought a few trinkets in the bazaar and had an Iranian lunch of lamb kebab served over long, thin rice kernels. Later that afternoon we visited the home of the Goodpastures, an American family whom we had met at the square dance. Mr. Goodpasture was building barracks for Iranian soldiers under the auspices of the U.S. Army Corps of Engineers. The family graciously served tea and showed us slides before we returned to the hotel and prepared to leave for the airport. Our flight was scheduled to depart at 9 the next morning.

Ariana Airlines phoned early to say we would leave an hour later...and then called again to report that they were delaying until the following day. We tried to find more interesting places to visit in Persia (the ancient name for Iran), but learned that the only other city of interest was Isfahan, located 211 miles to the south.

Isfahan is on the ancient north-south, east-west trade routes crossing Persia and was once one of the largest and most important cities in the world. It had become the capital of Persia in the 16th century and was still famous for its Islamic architecture, boulevards, covered bridges and palaces, as well as its mosques and minarets.

Although it sounded intriguing, we could not go there because it would take three days by car or would cost $36 to fly – an extravagance that we could not afford.

"Driving is mad!" I exclaimed, "It gets worse the further east we travel. No one pays any attention to the police; in fact they even fight with them." We concluded that at least Tehran maintained its streets reasonably well and the future looked hopeful because new construction was going up in many different areas.

Shah Mohammad Reza Pahlavi maintained six palaces, one for each member of his family. The Pahlavi dynasty was the ruling house of Iran from 1925 until 1979 when the Iranian Revolution occurred, abolished the monarchy and initiated an entirely new era.

The Shah, who originally established the dynasty in 1925, lasted until 1941 when he abdicated after the Anglo Soviet invasion during World War II. His son, the last Shah of Iran, succeeded him and was the monarch in power during our visit. Mohammad Reza Pahlavi died in exile in 1980 in Cairo, Egypt at the age of 60.

The local language was Farsi, very different from Arabic, although the letters in the two languages are similar. We learned that there were many Communists in Tehran, all of whom were operating underground and had come across the border from Iraq. We did not encounter any, at least that we knew of.

We discovered that the flight delay was because Ariana could not fly over Iraq due to the recent uprising, the same reason they would not allow us to enter their country. They rerouted the plane over Kuwait and Saudi Arabia and therefore it would arrive in Tehran later that afternoon, more than 24 hours after the scheduled landing. They explained that we could not fly into Kandahar, Afghanistan (a fuel stop before Kabul), as planned, because that airport did not have landing lights and could not accommodate night arrivals.

When we arrived at the Tehran airport two days later at 5:30 in the morning, we went straight to the Ariana desk. We attempted to seek reimbursement for our hotel bill, since it was much higher than we expected due to the delayed flights. Our efforts were unsuccessful, however. Once again, we were dealing with a different set of standards; we stretched our patience to respect their way of conducting business that was so foreign to us.

While I was biding my time in Tehran, I realized that it had been a long time since I had written home and so composed a letter to my Mother. I recently discovered the letter in my treasure trove of items in my old trunk.

Here it is, just as I wrote it…

January 23, 1959
Tehran, Iran

Dear Mother,

I bet you are amazed to see this heading! Our time in the Middle East and the holy land was so busy I had no time to write so now I will tell you the whole story as there isn't that much to see in Tehran and our next flight keeps being delayed so I have some spare time.

It all happened this way: As you know we stayed in Beirut, Lebanon for about two weeks trying to find a cheap way out, as we were not allowed to enter Iraq and take the boat to Pakistan. We spent our time trying to investigate every possible way that we could continue our trip around the world. Jane and I went to the harbor where we knocked on doors of shipping offices to try to get information. This must have been a shock for the office workers, as women do not go out of their houses here without a male accompanying them. In fact, the sight of four young girls in western dress probably blew their minds.

After trying several companies, we finally found someone who would at least listen to our plight. We met a very nice 47-year-old bachelor named Mike Haddad who helped us immensely. He immediately took us in hand, invited us to his apartment for drinks and dinner, and introduced us to his friends. Mike

asked where we were staying and said since the
Jerusalem House was very close to his apartment he
would appreciate a ride home. This turned out to be
fortuitous as he noticed that our car was idling too
slow and frequently stalling out. He opened the hood,
adjusted the throttle and solved our problem.

Mike found a way in which we could sail from
Beirut to Karachi for $200 each. In the meantime, we
were faced with selling the car, as shipping costs were
prohibitive. We had investigated the sale in Damascus
and learned that the cost of customs was very high,
more than the car was worth. We learned that the
situation was the same in Lebanon but one of Mike's
friends contacted his brother-in-law in Jerusalem,
Jordan who said he would buy the car for 200 pounds
sterling or $560. We decided to go there and sell it as
we had planned to visit Jerusalem anyway.

Just to catch up I have to tell you that Sue is
no longer with us. She is remaining in Damascus
and plans to marry Adnan. This brings to mind a
thought—she does not yet know whether she will be
married here or at her home in Michigan. In any case,
Adnan wants to go back to the states for further study
(he is a lawyer) and they will have to apartment hunt.
I told Sue that if she goes through New York she should
go to see you. This is irrelevant but she is a very nice
girl and I have become very fond of her.

To get back to the subject, while staying at the
Jerusalem House we were looking for a fourth for

*bridge while killing time before one of our many dinner
dates when a tall American boy walked in. He said he
had taken a year off from his studies at M.I.T. to travel
and had spent the summer in Afghanistan picking cashew nuts. Sue recognized him immediately as he lived
in Flint, Michigan and was the son of a well-known
millionaire. His name is Stewart Mott, not apple
juice; his father is Chairman of the Board of General
Motors. Stewart told us that he planned to return to
Afghanistan. When we told him of our plans to drive
to Jerusalem the next day he asked if he might come
along. We eagerly agreed as he could help pay for car
expenses and it would be more fun as we were getting a
little bored with each other.*

*We rushed around all morning obtaining visas
and emptying all our crap from the car. The only place
we could leave our stuff was with our friend Mike. By
the way he is hysterical – a real old maid. He is very
fastidious about his apartment but a very good guy.
He invited me to dinner at his place and I had a grand
time and lots of drinks. A full dinner was brought
in – white wine and all and just for me. He never eats
dinner and never leaves his apartment after 6:30 p.m.,
just a few more of his old maid quirks. Anyway, he
took quite a fancy to me, asking me to stay on with him
saying he would take me to the Far East or any place I
wanted to go. I naturally refused but he was very kind
and sincere.*

*We finally left Beirut at about 2 p.m. and drove back
to Damascus because we had to pass through Syria*

to get to Jordan. The border guards had become quite familiar since we had been back and forth over this route so many times. When they saw us coming, they threw up their hands in welcome and invited us in for coffee. They could not understand our association with Stewart but took him in like a member of the family. I nearly wet my pants laughing while posing for group pictures. The trip took about four hours as usual – two hours driving and an hour spent socializing at each border station. We had our ninth flat tire along the way, which Stewart happily changed.

We arrived in Damascus to find that Sue and Adnan were visiting our American friends, the Blakes. They are very nice folks; they insisted that all four of us spend the night at their home. They had just two spare rooms so Stewart and I were roommates. We left the next morning for Jerusalem.

Just outside of Damascus, the desert began – the most barren place I have ever seen. The soil was very red and claylike, covered with rocks-you could not imagine anything growing there. Sometimes the rocks were piled in strange little stacks, sometimes outlining a small plot. It looked as if the people had nothing to else to do but move rocks around. We have become used to the look of the people but they would amaze you. The women wear veils and the men's heads are covered by towel-like headgear. Of course there are camel caravans wandering all over and you can just imagine how thrilled I was to see them! We often have to stop the car while they cross. Again we had fun at the border crossing, a new one this time but we got the usual coffee invitation.

As we drove further the land became more barren, dusty and dirty, a true desert. We passed through Amman, Jordan, and saw nothing more than mud huts. We then took a very good new road which led us past the Dead Sea (1300 feet below sea level). It looks somewhat like the Grand Canyon – it was really funny to just keep going down, down, and down to the sea but more about that later.

About five kilometers outside of Jerusalem we ran out of gas – usual trick for us – we added a full Jerry can which we took from our trunk, drove a few more feet and the car gave out. Right away people stopped to ask if they could help, I must say Arab hospitality is fantastic, not a single car went by without stopping to see if they could help. Finally, we found a truck driver who knew a thing or two about motors and told us that there was water in the gas line. He worked on it for three hours, even went into town to get spare parts. He had been working for three days and nights straight, driving his truck but would not quit until the repair was complete. We told the truck driver that we were going to sell the car and he said he thought we should get about 300 pounds for it. We tried to pay him for his repair work, but he would not accept any money. Instead he insisted we follow him into Bethlehem where he knew of a good cheap hotel.

We accepted his offer and then came the laughs. Bethlehem is lovely but has not changed in 2000 years

*– not even the plumbing system (a hole in the ground).
Stew and I went to look for hotel accommodations.
They showed us a large room filled with six dirty beds
but the people were kind and it was indeed cheap so we
said we would take it. The truck driver and his helper
were staying there also. We figured they would take
the other two beds but as it turned out, they slept in
another room.*

*Bethlehem is a lovely little town in its own way –
truly silent and peaceful, built on the side of a hill and
exactly the same as the Christmas carol describes.*

*The next morning we got up at seven in order to
make the eight o'clock service at the Church of the
Nativity, the place where Christ was born. First, there
was a Greek Orthodox ceremony followed by a Catholic
one in the grotto where the birth took place.*

*We went on into Jerusalem and looked up a man
who owned a travel office and had been recommended
by the manager of Jerusalem House. He was very kind
and suggested we take his guide for one half day as he
would give us half off the regular price ($140). The
guide turned out to be a tall, skinny Arab who spoke
English very well and who knew an awful lot about the
area. We felt it necessary to have a guide and we split
the price between the four of us.*

*He showed us around for the rest of the day and
became our best friend. When we told him we planned
to sell the car he said he had at least six friends who
would give us their money immediately. When we
drove around, people began bargaining, rushing up*

*to us and offering better and better prices. The crowd
grew and grew to the point where they were stopping
us along the street pushing wads of dollar bills in our
faces. We had trouble fighting them off.*

*Some friends of Zachariah (the guide) invited us
out to THE one and only nightspot in Jerusalem. This
was nice of them but we had spent the last four weeks
going out every night to THE best nightclub in town
dancing up a storm with the Arabs. Anyway, we
accepted and set out with a large bargaining crowd
following us. The bargainers stood at the bar because
we told them we would not talk business in the evening.
Arab men appeared from all parts of the room asking
us to dance – one invited me out to the new racy
Dead Sea Hotel the next evening, another invited me to
lunch as he slipped his card in my hand. Overall,
it was a gay evening.*

*Stewart and Zach were both with us; probably
a good thing since I now understand more about that
part of the world. We insisted on leaving at about
1 a.m. and returned to our four-bed hotel room.*

*I must digress here to give you some idea of the
charming living conditions we were experiencing. Johns
are holes in the ground, never any more or less. Actually,
they are more smelly and horrible than you could ever
imagine. Once you get the knack of it, though, you are
ok. Just squat over the hole and make sure you have some
Kleenex soaked with cheap perfume to hold over your*

nose. I never thought I could do it but it is amazing what you can do when you have to.

The next morning four different sets of prospective buyers hammered at our door at 8 a.m. Zach arrived soon after and walked right into the room as did all the rest and we continued to do business from the bedside. We spent the rest of the morning bargaining and finally met the brother-in-law who had originally offered to buy the car. He raised his price from 200 dinar to 265, which translates to $750 dollars. If you remember, we bought it for $700 so we were pretty happy. They let us use the car for the afternoon so we set out for Jericho where we visited the famous wall. Jericho is a true oasis in the desert, palm trees and all. We also saw the River Jordan and went down to the Dead Sea where Jane and Stewart swam. The water was very dirty looking, the waves small and very, very salty – more so than Salt Lake as I remember it.

When we drove, back into Jerusalem all our friends flowed out into the streets to invite us to the Dead Sea Hotel. We declined as we had promised to go to the brother-in-law's for a few drinks and to settle papers. Meanwhile our friends followed us to the hotel and had drinks right up until the brother-in-law called for us. All went well that evening and we left the next morning for Amman to settle customs matters and turn over the car. We travelled back to Damascus and Beirut by taxi.

*Meanwhile (if your eyes aren't giving out) a few
comments on the people and situation here in the
Middle East. There is, of course, a horribly strong
anti-Israel feeling – so much so that when we applied
for Jordanian visas in Brussels we were required to
have affidavits proving that we were not Jewish.
If you have been to Israel and have that stamp on
your passport, they will not permit you to enter an
Arab country.*

*I guess you know a lot more about the situation
than I do, but I never realized quite what a beating the
Arabs took by the division of Palestine. They have been
given all the worst land; it is obvious that it is almost
impossible to cultivate the soil. The many, many
refugees were forced to flee from their homes with
literally no more than the clothes on their backs.
People are sitting idle in the streets – there is no work
for them. We also saw many refugee camps – people
living in miserable mud huts in worse poverty than
I could have imagined. Most of the people we have
met in the Middle East are Palestinian refugees. Our
friends have been the well-to-do ones but they have
their struggles as well.*

*I do not mean to go overboard on this but I look
back and recall how little publicity they have had at
home. All I can remember is advertising for the United
Jewish Appeal. Anyway, the people do not harp on the
subject but just say that they hope someday America
will understand the problem and at least know that*

they are not all barbarians living in tents. Enough of that, but it has been very interesting here – I am really glad to have spent so much time in the Middle East.

Now, back at the ranch, in the small world of our plans, earthshaking things were happening – that night we spent in Damascus with the Blakes we talked to Stew about Afghanistan and learned that it would be cheaper for us to get to Pakistan and India by plane than by boat. It also seemed to be a lot more interesting as the ship would only stop at Aqaba and Karachi. The next morning we decided to go by way of Afghanistan so we sent a cable cancelling the boat reservation. The plane (Ariana Afghan Airways) was scheduled to leave Thursday so we had to be back in Beirut on Tuesday – get Iranian visas Wednesday and clear out all our belongings in order to leave at 8 a.m. the following day.

We stopped at Damascus on the way back, said goodbye to Sue and took another taxi to Beirut. These taxis cost about $250 each for a four to six hour drive. Our budget was still tight but we could afford it as we had sold the car. Again, we got a huge reception at the border and were told that the security (Syrian) police had been there asking questions about us. This leads to another long, involved chapter so I think I will be writing all night – hope you can bear up under it.

You doubtless got the idea that they were censoring my letters. There was very little I could explain but we (Gloria and I) got involved in a real cloak and dagger situation.

*During the second week of our stay in Damascus,
Gloria and I stopped by to see the Blakes after tennis.
He is working with the AFME (American Friends
of the Middle East), an organization that helps with
exchange students, etc. We had a good time – ended
up having dinner and spending the night. They said
there is nothing much to do in Damascus so they stay
up every night until about 5 a.m. and sleep until noon.
We just talked and had a very good time.*

*About a week later, one of the best players in
Syria, a bachelor about 38, invited us to play tennis.
He did not actually play because he said he had
injured his arm. Nevertheless, we became friends and
he invited us to his friends' home for tea. The friends
were also very nice, a Hungarian woman and her
Syrian husband. Everyone spoke French. They had an
interesting story to relate but I can't go into that now.
They invited us to tennis every afternoon; called for us
at 3 and sat on a bench talking while we played. They
arranged for us to meet many good players (my game
improved immensely) and they took us to tea afterward.
They invited us out many evenings for fun and
interesting meals.*

*Finally, Adnan told us that we had to stop seeing
them. They were all members of a political party that
was plotting to overthrow the UAR; in fact, they had
already assassinated a general. He told us that the
Minister of the Interior had summoned him to explain
our actions. The Minister told Adnan that they had*

followed Gloria and me ever since the evening we spent
with the Blakes – they knew virtually every step we
had taken and would not extend our visas. Adnan
warned that this might have repercussions for us in the
U.S. Understand, of course, that we were just as
innocent as can be but could see how we could raise
their suspicions. The more we talked the more Gloria
and I began to understand that it all added up.

This sounds like an exciting story and in fact, it
was. You may think that I am getting a little carried
away but we ended up with proof. We were in a very
bad position as we liked these people and could not
abruptly refuse all dates we had already accepted. At
the same time we did not want to do anything that
would be harmful to Sue and Adnan.

We finally settled it all by paying a sneak visit to
our friends one night but noticed that two men were
following us in a car. When we arrived, the Hungarian
woman gave us each a very nice gift (jewelry). This
became very exciting as we surreptitiously made
our way through the dark rainy streets at night. We
breathed a collective sigh of relief when we finally got
out of Syria unscathed.

The payoff to the whole deal came when we
returned from Jordan. When we arrived at the Syrian
border, our friend the guard said that the security
police had been asking about us. Once again, luck
was on our side. We told him that we would return
on Tuesday but he misunderstood and told the police

*we would return on Thursday. Anyway, we got out.
There are more details that I can explain when I see you
but it sure was an adventure to end all adventures.*

*I hope this letter reaches you as I would hate to
have to relate it all again. Save it though, as I will
probably enjoy reading it in my old age. Also, please
don't talk about it as I am still not sure what was at the
bottom of it all.*

*We returned to Beirut the next day, sorted and
repacked our belongings. Mike is sending a box home
to you by slow freight. It includes all three of our
belongings that we want to keep but cannot carry.
They will notify you when it arrives in N.Y. in about
two months. I would appreciate it if you could pick it up.*

*Just to make matters worse, they changed our
departure from 8 a.m. to 2 a.m. Thursday so we spent
the last evening before having a gay party at Mike's.
He was very worried about our plan and insisted that
I send postcards every day. He said if he does not hear
he will send out the international police. Do not let
this worry you – we will be fine as we are checking in
at the American embassies en route and are taking all
necessary precautions.*

*We boarded the old plane, (9 passengers mostly
freight, a hole in the door and just a bare fuselage with
a few seats). It was a fine flight – over Baghdad at
night then over desolate, wild mountains.*

*We arrived in Tehran in the morning and I spent
24 hours in bed as I was tired and hung over after a*

strenuous four weeks. Tehran is nothing but mud. Once again, friends have appeared from nowhere and we have dates every evening. We go out together at all times for safety's sake. Am still fine and having a fantastic time. My only complaint is that I have a bad knee. I'll try to keep you informed. I hope all is well and that you don't go blind from reading this book.

Love to all.

Me

CHAPTER TWENTY THREE
Kabul, Afghanistan
January 30, 1959

We boarded the Ariana flight and noticed that a curtain
separated the baggage/freight section from the passengers.
We again stuffed rags in the faulty door and turned one of the
seats around so that we could play bridge. I wondered if the
plane would make it to Kabul and feared that perhaps we were
taking one too many chances.

We flew for six hours over barren, brown desert seeing no
signs of any human habitation. It resembled my image of the
surface of the moon. The mountain ranges looked like a relief
map rising abruptly from the flat land. Everything was barren
and brown since it was the dead of winter.

The Kandahar airport was a cleared field surrounded by a
sunny valley. We chatted with the pilot and copilot under the
shade of the wing while they refueled the plane. During the

refueling they discovered a mechanical problem in the aircraft
and so we had to stay overnight in a nearby Quonset hut while
repairs were made.

The next leg of the journey was the most interesting. We flew
low over beautiful snowcapped mountains in order to save fuel.
As we approached Kabul we saw the foothills of the Hindu
Kush, a sub range of the Himalayas. We spotted several villages,
groups of brown mud huts surrounded by walls. It was plain
that these people had been experiencing tribal warfare for
centuries and therefore needed the protection of the walls.

We landed at Kabul Airport – once again a field full of
potholes. The airport was a great distance from the city and so
we took a public bus into town. Men with Mongolian features,
wearing long robes and turbans on their heads, filled most
seats in the bus. Some of them were barefoot despite the cold
winter weather. There were no women in sight.

When we finally came across some women we noticed that
they were dressed in *chadri* – shrouds that covered their bodies
from head to foot. Their outfits were ghostlike veils in blue,
brown and black. They had only slits for eyeholes, so that the
woman could see out but no one could see in.

We arrived in Kabul but were not able to find a local taxi
with a large enough trunk for our luggage, so we hired a
Russian model that was the largest one available. Stewart rode
on the front fender. The police soon stopped us and made
him move inside, so he sat on our laps.

Stewart directed the driver to the home of his friend
Dietrich Schnabel, a large German fellow who had established
a business in Kabul trading both dried fruit and wool. Dietrich
told us that it had taken him five years to make his business
viable as he had struggled to learn the language, customs, and
local ways, which were far different from those in Germany.
He called his American friend Laura Meyer, who was working
for ICA (International Cooperation Administration), and she
immediately offered to let us stay at her home.

The U.S. State Department Delegation of Authority established the ICA on June 30, 1955. This body coordinated foreign assistance programs for the U.S. for a short period until its abolishment in 1961.

In the late 1950s, the Afghans wanted to develop radio and television programming. Their progress in these media fields was made possible by the ICA, the Fulbright program and other American aid organizations. Ariana Afghan Airlines formed a partnership with Pan Am to train pilots, flight attendants, ground crews and airport staff for a growing network of international air routes as part of the alliance.

The U.S. had declined Afghanistan's request for defense cooperation but extended an economic assistance program focused on the development of the country's physical infrastructure: roads, dams, and power plants. Later U.S. aid shifted to technical assistance programs to develop the skills needed to build a modern economy. The U.S. focused on Afghanistan for a strategic purpose, mainly to counter the spread of communism into south Asia, particularly the Persian Gulf region.

Dietrich cautioned us about the threat of the white slave trade, which he said was very active in the area. He warned that we should never go outside alone, because many women had disappeared. He told us that it was common for Afghan men to spit on unveiled women and suggested that we cover our bodies as much as possible when in public.

We had not been aware of this threat and therefore were eager to ask more questions regarding the white slave trade. In our minds we were hoping that this was just a fictitious tale from some Arabian Nights saga in which they kidnapped women and took them to an Arab Sheik's harem for the rest of their lives. When Dietrich answered our questions, we became very unnerved to think that this could actually happen to us. As far as we were concerned, we had been invincible up to this point but for the first time, we questioned our ability to deal with such a threat.

We discussed the matter at length and decided that our only defense was for the four of us to stick close together, wear clothes that covered as much of our bodies as possible and to keep our eyes and ears sharp at all times. We took this threat very seriously and our concern remained primarily in our minds during our entire stay in Afghanistan.

Laura Meyer joined us after work and took us to her apartment. After dinner four young American men came over to meet us. They were working for Fairchild, a company that was doing mapping for an ICA project in that area. They had heard of our arrival earlier when one of the Pan Am agents radioed from Kandahar that three American girls would soon arrive in Kabul. Once again we found that news of our arrival travelled fast and I supposed it was a real treat for these young men to see three young American girls...a rarity in Afghanistan in those days!

These American men took us to town the next day so that we could buy warm coats and Karakul fur hats as we were freezing in the bitter cold winter conditions. The Karakul hats are triangular and made from the fur of an aborted lamb from the Qaraqul breed of sheep. I bought a yellow Yak skin coat decorated with bright red embroidery outside and a furry inside, which kept me very warm. (I wore that coat proudly for many years on skiing trips but after about 20 years, it finally disintegrated.)

After we lunched at their club, the young men took us to Istalif, a village about 18 miles northeast of Kabul, touted as one of the most beautiful places in the country. In midwinter, however, it was bleak. The Russians had built the well-paved road over which we travelled in a Land Rover. Everyone commented that the Russians produced very visible projects whereas the U.S. had poured their funds into projects such as technical assistance or dams and electric power plants far from the city and out of the sight of most Afghans.

Our American friends invited us to a party the following evening. Shortly after we arrived at the gathering of diplomats from many countries, we had six invitations to continue on to other parties. Indians, Russians, Afghans and Turks filled the room along with several American diplomats.

I met and danced with a man from the U.S. Embassy who told me something unnerving.

"Don't be stupid," he said, "You know why I am here. I am a security officer. I have a group of 10 guys with me. We have the whole place staked out. One of our men has his eyes on each of you girls at all times."

He went on to say, "You know what Teal (Gloria) is, with that nice innocent face – she's an agent." I thought he meant for the communists, which I figured was crazy, but he beat around the bush some more and finally said he thought she was "working for our team."

I excused myself and went to the restroom where I reported this to Gloria. She vehemently denied his theory and assured me that this was not true, adding that I knew her well enough to know that if that had been the case she would have shared it with me since we were such close friends by that time. It did, however, plant a seed of doubt in my mind when I considered how well travelled she was and how much expertise she had acquired in the ins and outs of foreign travel

One thing was for certain, we were all more and more nervous as we kept hearing of "disappearances." When I returned to the party, the embassy official told me he had called the Marines for extra protection, as he feared there were too many Afghan men present. The Marines arrived and immediately escorted us home. In addition to all this intrigue, several fights broke out during the course of the party. Despite all this, I had a terrific evening. We were willing to leave with the marine escorts that evening, as the threat of the white slave trade loomed heavy over our heads.

The next day we went skiing in the nearby mountains. We drove 21 miles to the ski slope where we climbed to 8,000 ft. with our skis on our shoulders. The arduous climb became

more and more difficult as we ascended into the thinner air,
but fortunately youth was on our side and our indomitable
determination helped us place each difficult step in front of
the other. By the time we reached the top we needed a long
rest before putting on our skis for the exhilarating trip down
the slope.

We filled the next few days with errands and activities.
We went to the Pakistan, Indian and Indonesian embassies to
arrange for our visits. We found a dispensary where we secured
world health cards and immunizations against both cholera
and typhus. I rode horses with Eckhart, Dietrich's business
partner. We sped to and from the stable on his motorcycle
over well-paved roads. Although he was a very cautious driver,
I wondered what my poor mother would say if she could see
me on the back of that vehicle. We were frequently wined and
dined in the homes of international diplomats. Everyone was
anxious to meet the three American girls, a most unusual sight
in this outpost of the world.

I preferred Kabul to Tehran, but clearly did not want to live
in either place. There were ditches or open channels in the
streets where water was sweeping along with assorted garbage
and even drainage from household sewage systems. We had
seen many beggars, some of whom were purposely maimed.
Only 50% of children born in Afghanistan survived at that
time. We were surprised at how primitive the country was.

We continued on to Pakistan by hitching a free ride on a
British mail lorry (truck), which left Kabul each week bound
for Peshawar. Little did we know that we would rely on the
skills of the driver every bit as much as we had upon our airline
pilots when we entered this treacherous mountain gorge. We
thanked Laura for having hosted us for two weeks and bade
goodbye as we set out for one of the more hair-raising
adventures of our trip.

We had learned a lot during our visit to this harsh country
and gained an understanding of how the centuries of tribal

struggles along with the rugged terrain in the foothills of the Himalaya had resulted in such a brutal society. They were still stoning women to death in the city square for committing adultery and chopping off the right hand of a thief. Women were property and had no rights.

We boarded the van after sunset to begin our overnight journey through the renowned Khyber Pass in Pakistan, a drop in elevation of more than 3,000 feet. We made the passage at night so that they could deliver the mail in the early morning. Gloria and I elected to go first as they could only take two passengers on that trip. Stewart and Jane offered to stay behind and take the next available lorry. Gloria and I sat side by side in one of the two rows of seats behind the driver. We shared tuna fish sandwiches that we had brought for our dinner. For the first hour our view was obscured by blinding snowfall.

The fact that we were traveling in the dark was both a disappointment and a blessing as we passed many beautiful areas and stunning vistas...but also treacherous terrain and precipitous curves. We could hear a roaring stream somewhere hundreds of feet down below. The narrow winding road led to a tunnel at the top where we exited the vehicle and saw what we could of a sweeping panorama. Meanwhile we cringed as the thundering of unseen falling rocks and boulders pounded in our ears.

Our fellow passenger Dick Kountze, who was working for the Asian Foundation, had travelled this route many times. He explained how threatening it could be in such wet weather. He told us that often the lorry was blocked by the falling rocks and had to wait long hours until help arrived. Since it had been raining and snowing all night, we became even more apprehensive.

Dick told us tales of his travels in the outlying areas of Kabul and spoke of a Swedish girl who a religious fanatic stabbed in the marketplace. Fortunately, her father who was a skilled physician saved her life. She later had the choice of having the crazed man killed, killing him herself or having him imprisoned for life for punishment. She chose to have him turned over to the custody of his family. We each breathed a sigh of relief that we were safely making it out of Afghanistan and crossed our fingers that we would live through this scary road trip.

Despite the tension, the driver did a fantastic job, it was evident that he had made this trip many times and was a very competent driver. I could not shut my eyes for a moment because it was too exciting. When the snow stopped, we could see thrilling and terrifying surroundings as we navigated hairpin turns carved around huge boulders. When we came upon large rocks in the road, we got out and helped move them aside.

We made our way that night over more than 140 miles along a road that dropped off many thousands of feet into the steep gorge below. It was probably fortunate that we passed the area in darkness as the road was muddy, filled with ruts and precipitously hugged the edge of the mountain.

We crossed over a large suspension bridge that swayed in the wind and buckled as our van slowly made its way across. When we arrived at the Afghan checkpoint, it was just after midnight. We slept in the van until 6 a.m. when the officers returned to duty and allowed us to proceed.

Three miles into Pakistan we arrived at the famous Khyber Pass, which connects Afghanistan to Pakistan, cutting through the northeastern part of the Spin Ghar Mountains. This was an integral part of the ancient Silk Road and is one of the oldest known passes in the world at an altitude of 3,510 ft. The views at this point were as spectacular as earlier in the journey.

The Khyber Rifles, named for the pass, is a para military force forming a part of the Pakistani Army. During British rule they recruited members from tribesmen of the northwest frontier to guard the pass.

As we drove along this route in pounding rain, a cold wind was blowing our vehicle from side to side. Small fortresses guarded each hill as they have done for centuries. This road

was paved and made for a comfortable ride in the lorry at last.
We passed shepherds herding their flocks and even saw a camel
trail alongside the road.

The land looked richly fertile and well cultivated in the
lower regions while high, snow covered mountains loomed
in the distance. Overall, it took about one hour to travel the
famous pass while the entire trip was more than eight hours.
At the bottom of the pass, the terrain became very flat and
boggy. At one point, we forded a small river and came upon a
herd of water buffalo as we climbed the opposite embankment.

I could hardly believe that I had just weathered one of the
world's most difficult routes in an overnight ride in a British
mail lorry! The whole concept boggled my mind and left me
utterly exhausted mentally and physically from bracing myself
through the treacherous curves.

Above: Zachariah, Jane and Stewart stand beside the Dead Sea

Below: Jane, Gloria, Stewart wearing Karakul hats and our hostess Laura Meyer

page 127
Above right: Gloria on main street in Istalif, Afghanistan

Middle: Gloria riding in horse drawn cart with Jane standing alongside in Kabul

Below: Passengers standing in shelter of wing during fuel stop in Kandahar

Above: Gloria with me in my Yak coat on ski outing in Afghanistan

Right: I loved riding horses in Kabul

CHAPTER TWENTY FOUR
Lahore, West Pakistan
February 5, 1959

After we left the Khyber Pass, we found that the architecture became far more interesting. We no longer saw mud huts but houses with small hand hewn decorations beside the front doors.

We reached Peshawar the next morning at about 10. Peshawar is the capital and the largest city in the Khyber Province, nestled in a large valley near the eastern end of the pass. "The City on the Frontier" is centrally located at the crossroads of central and south Asia.

We unloaded our luggage in our van-mate Dick's room at the Dean Hotel. Gloria and I had tea with Erick and Mr. Hamidullah at their used car establishment. We had met these Pakistani men at the Fair and they told us that they would be delighted to welcome us to their country.

Gloria mentioned that she would like to see a Khyber Rifle. The two men immediately sent an errand boy out to fetch one. We learned that the term "Khyber Rifle" not only referred to a certain special firearm but to the military force that used it as well.

As it turned out, a rifle by that name was often more correctly a "Khyber Pass Copy" – or a firearm manufactured by cottage gunsmiths in the Khyber Pass region. Artisans there have long had a reputation for producing unlicensed, homemade copies of firearms using whatever materials were available; often they were made from train rails, scrap motor vehicles and any other materials that had been abandoned.

Our two Pakistani friends guided us through a local museum and into town to shop. We saw many striking tables and other furniture items inlaid with ivory, beautifully hand-painted. We were not able to buy any of these items for which Pakistan was famous because our funds barely allowed us to subsist. Mr. Hamidullah very kindly gave us each a handkerchief.

By this point in the trip Gloria and I had become good friends. We had met and travelled together in Brussels and had the same interests. Jane and Stewart often went off together to visit the many places he had discovered in his previous stay and they seemed to have a good time together.

Although the weather was still rainy and cold, Peshawar seemed like a paradise with its orange trees, flowers, palms and lush greenery. We had bathed in Dick's hotel room before he took us to dinner and on to the station to catch our train that evening. It had been a grueling day and night covering rough roads and steep terrain, so we were relieved to be traveling by train for a change.

Gloria and I shared a compartment with a nice looking middle-aged Indian lady and her shy niece who were on their way to Bombay. The girl's mother was living in the North Country, which had become the new country of Pakistan, the British Indian Empire petitioned it in 1947.

After gaining independence from British Colonialism, the citizens of Pakistan physically divided it into two enclaves. On July 1, 1970 West Pakistan was renamed Pakistan. In 1971 the

former East Pakistan declared independence and was renamed
Bangladesh. It borders on India to its west, north, and east
and Burma (now named Myanmar) to its southeast and by the
Bay of Bengal to the south.

I slept like a log on the train as I was suffering from a bad
cold and was still recovering from the long night of travel.
The thoughtful Indian lady bought us tea in the morning at a
station stop. She provided a kind and gentle introduction to
another harsh country whose ways were foreign to us.

When we arrived in Lahore thin dark men working as
bearers or porters were available to help with our luggage. We
secured "retiring rooms" in the station, which were clean and
adequate at a cost of only $1 per night.

A *tonga* (horse drawn carriage) carried us to a public
relations office where we met with Mr. Isiz. He provided us
with information about the area and asked us to meet him for
a newspaper interview at 6 p.m. It seemed, once again, that we
were newsworthy visitors. This was one of many interviews
and photographs displayed in local newspapers along our way.

We visited the famous Shalimar Gardens, a Muslim garden
complex that was built in 1641. Mr. Isiz toured us through the
city where we saw beautiful, large houses that reminded me of
elegant homes I had seen in Florida. We found this new part
of the city to be quite a contrast to the abject poverty evident
in the old city.

The following day we visited the Fort next to Shalimar
Gardens. This was built during the brilliant Mughal civilization
which reached its height during the reign of Emperor Shah
Jahan from 1592-1666. The Fort contains marble palaces and
mosques ornately decorated with mosaics and gilt. The Mughals
built the gardens on three terraces with lodges, waterfalls and
oriental ponds. They are unequalled in their beauty.

The Fort included the palace of the Shah. I concluded
that this beautiful area probably represented the origin of the
formal garden, as we know it today.

We returned by public bus through the old part of the city where we passed a band of gypsies tending their naked children. The adults were sitting around picking lice from each other's heads. The children answered nature's call anywhere in the street, having no encumbrance such as pants to remove.

We saw beggars, many of whom were deformed. My journal entry recorded, *"...sacred cows that were a gray color roaming about freely. All the animals and people are so skinny that you can almost see every bone in their body."* We noticed little girls aged five or six who were carrying their baby sisters and brothers while the parents did whatever they could to survive.

We checked in at the U.S. Consulate and received a cable from Jane and Stewart reporting that they had been snowed in. Apparently, we made it out just in time.

Gloria and I returned to the railroad depot in time to depart for Amritsar, a city in the northern Punjab state of India that is 15 miles east of the Pakistan border and a major commercial, cultural, and transportation center as well as the center of Sikhism.

We continued our second-class journey across India to New Delhi and shared a compartment with a very nice man who said he regretted that he had not known we were coming as we could have stayed with his family. Once again, we met with nothing but kind and hospitable people. His family soon joined us in the compartment, giggled, and stared at us for the remainder of the trip.

Gloria and I slept as best we could on the hard wooden bench provided to second-class passengers. The accommodations were far different and more uncomfortable than anything I had experienced at home. We ate the food that we bought at depot stops but for safety reasons limited ourselves to only items that could be peeled or shelled, such as bananas or nuts.

Unfortunately I have a horrible aversion to bananas – so I existed on cashew nuts which were cheap because they were grown nearby.

CHAPTER TWENTY FIVE
Reunited
New Delhi, India
February 7, 1959

In order to kill time we had tea in the New Delhi station at six the next morning before going to the American Express office that did not open until 10. American Express was the only way in which we could keep in touch with our friends and relatives and so we eagerly checked in at each city. We had given out itineraries so that they could send letters ahead for our collection upon arriving.

As we stepped up to the mail counter and spoke our names one-by-one, we were very often met with an "Oh yes" — a welcome comment at each stop. I was thrilled to find that I had 15 letters waiting, including a check from my aunt for $50, which was a fortune to me at the time. Our spirits always lifted when we received news from home.

We registered at the local YWCA that offered accommodations for $2 a day including meals. Much to our surprise and joy, we found Sue waiting for us. We rushed toward her and greeted our lost companion with hugs. She had called off the engagement and joined us once again for the rest of the journey. We were all thrilled to have her back on board as our little group of friends had become cohesive and we had been feeling a huge gap in her absence. Sue did not share the details of what had transpired to cause her decision, but we did not press her. We were just glad to have her back.

"India is wonderful," I told Sue, "filled with warm sun, beautiful flowers and trees. But there are thousands of people all over the streets, many of whom are beggars who are maimed and deformed."

This was the beginning of our driving desire to get away from crowds. When we went into the streets, people would crowd around staring and pressing so close that they would lean against us. We became annoyed as time went on and the throngs became more and more brazen and persistent.

The next morning we went to the Red Fort that had been the residence of the Mughal emperors of India for nearly 200 years. It is located in the center of Delhi and houses a number of museums. In addition to accommodating the emperors and their households, the Red Fort was the ceremonial and political center of Mughal government. They built it in 1648 and named it for the massive enclosing walls of red sandstone.

The fort is the main tourist attraction of the capital city of Delhi and encompasses 17 stunning buildings. The exteriors are shining white marble with lovely delicate carved designs intricately inlaid with precious stones. The bathroom is a series of enclosures containing pools filled with either hot or cold water. A gully running with cool water courses through the interior supplying an amazing version of air conditioning.

We walked under the massive, extending limbs of a large tree and looked up to see that it was filled with chattering mon-

keys running wild through the branches and down into
the walkways. They were sacred creatures in Indian culture
and could wander freely.

We went to a government tourist agency where we gathered
more information to be sure we did not miss any of the
important sights. The manager asked us to return later that
afternoon so that he could take our pictures to send to our
hometown newspapers. We continued on to the Reserve Bank
of India where they told us that we could pick up our refund
from the British India Steamship Company, owners of the ship
from Basrah. Once again, they turned us away and said that we
could get the refund when we reached Calcutta.

We visited the American Embassy, a beautiful white stucco
building with a lacework wall screening a cooling pool and
fountain. An American lady took us on a tour of the building
which included a visit to the well-appointed Ambassador's
office. Every Embassy we saw in these far-flung countries
was impressive…and did a good job of putting America's best
foot forward.

I summed up this leg of the journey in my diary by saying,
*"New Delhi is beautiful. There are many modern buildings
that vary greatly in style and architecture."* The city was only
26 years old; it became the new capital on February 13, 1931.

We boarded another train that night for Ajmer, again second
class, and would be sleeping yet again on a hard wooden bench
in the usual dirty, crowded compartment. These train trips were
becoming more and more tiresome as we sat for long hours on
the uncomfortable benches and found very little edible food at
the station stops.

Although some of our fellow passengers were friendly,
most of them stared at us relentlessly and seemed to have no
respect for personal space. The weather was unbearably hot;
open windows exposed us to a constant barrage of dust and
dirt. The hours passed slowly and we all agreed that riding on
a second-class train in India was the pits.

CHAPTER TWENTY SIX
Ajmer, India
February 11, 1959

The doctors Hall met us when we arrived in Ajmer early the
next morning. They were both physicians and colleagues. I
have no idea who these doctors were all these years later or how
we had met them…but they were expecting us and graciously
were planning to put us up in their home. I guess it was another
of our fortunate Brussels acquaintances that we had so carefully
made while planning the trip.

The doctors' driver seemed to have some strange disease
because we noticed that large warts covered his entire body.
The man seemed to be in reasonably good health other than the
strange skin condition, no doubt the result of some incurable
disease. We were taken to "The Domes," the home of the
doctors, where we bathed and ate a real breakfast – a treat after
so much depot food.

They later drove us around the area so that we could enjoy the beautiful countryside. This region was a true Garden of Eden compared to the crowded cities we had experienced thus far in India. We saw a handsome temple on the bank of a cooling blue lake amidst this lush, green, mountainous setting. The doctors explained that the lake dries up every summer in the unbearable 115-degree heat.

Our hosts escorted us to a friend's home for tea and later to the TB (tuberculosis) sanatorium where they worked. The large complex was made up of many whitewashed buildings, all constructed of mud. They showed us an occupational therapy building, a nurse's residence, wards, operating rooms, separate areas for recovery and recreation and a chapel. We even observed a lung surgery in progress. I could not help but cringe at the sight of a large hole in the patient's chest, exposing his lung.

The doctors took us to see Pusha, a sacred village beside a lake where local people wash away all their sins. We passed camels, sacred cows, peacocks and monkeys along our drive. When we entered the village, beggars were squatting along the narrow road with hands outstretched. We visited the Temple of Brahma, which featured a fertility shrine where people prayed that they would conceive babies.

In the distant field, we spotted a band of vultures feasting on some creature's remains. They told us that in the Parsi religion people take their dead to a tower and lay them out for the vultures to consume as an act of purification. The remaining bones drop down into a well.

These two doctors had been practicing in Ajmer for 18 years. The female Dr. Hall's main interest was in family planning. She explained to us that the difficulty was not in getting the women to use contraceptives but rather finding a place for them to keep these devices. She said that the families all live together in one room mud huts and that the women have no personal space in which to store their belongings.

She went on to say that most babies are conceived in the field when the wife goes out to take her husband lunch.

Dr. Hall added that in many cases they deliberately maim the children so that they can become beggars that are more effective. She told us this matter-of-factly, but we Americans looked at each other, faces in shock, appalled. We found this concept beyond imagination.

CHAPTER TWENTY SEVEN

Jaipur, India
February 12, 1959

On our way to Jaipur the next morning, our hosts took us
to see the Amber Fort of Rajasthan that sits high on the crest
of a rugged hill. The Amber Fort was the ancient citadel of
the Kachhawa clan that ruled Amer before the capital of the
Rajasthan state shifted to Jaipur. The fort, known as the Amber
Palace, is located in the town of Amer, only 11 kilometers
from Jaipur.

We approached the impressive edifice and our first impression was one of fascination for the long, serpentine staircase
that wound up the steep hill. We ascended and passed many
elephants heading toward the Fort with their *howdahs* (saddles)
filled with tourists.

The Amber Fort is a fascinating blend of Hindu and Mughal
architecture built in white marble and red sandstone. It sits on

the edge of Maotha Lake, casting a captivating reflection when viewed from the far side of the lake.

We entered the first room and found thousands of mirrors set in the walls and ceilings. The intricate carving and inlay work in the marble was breathtaking. They explained that the servants transported the Maharani throughout the large palace in a human drawn rickshaw.

We went next door to the Rambagh palace, now a luxury hotel, where we enjoyed an elegant tea served in one of the newly renovated rooms.

The doctors drove us to a mobile medical unit parked in a nearby village square. We viewed the mobile unit as they described the equipment that the facility provided. We next went to the home of a Muslim family where the women greeted us and invited us to sit on small square stools. Dr. Hall explained that one of the women was suffering from syphilis and had given birth to eight children, only four of whom survived. She took us on to four more homes where she called on patients with various ailments. Throughout the area, goats and chickens roamed freely through the houses and grounds.

CHAPTER TWENTY EIGHT

Agra, India
February 18, 1959

We returned to New Delhi in order to continue southeast
to our next planned stop in Agra, the home of the famous Taj
Majal. The train ride back to Delhi was the most grueling yet.
We started out at 11:30 a.m. and did not arrive at our destination until eight that evening…covering a meager distance of
only 172 miles. Today the train trip takes four hours, half as
long as our trip in 1959.

We were third class passengers this time, something no
civilized person should ever attempt. At one point our small
compartment contained about 25 people who spent the whole
time staring at us and pressing closer, oblivious to our need for
personal space. None of us understood the others' language
and therefore we used only gestures to communicate. It seems
that deodorant had not been invented in this region and the
smell was pungent, to say the least.

Dust, dirt, and sweat covered our bodies by the end of
the trip so we checked in at the Hotel Rex next to the station
immediately. The cost ($2 per person) was prohibitive for us,
but we were in desperate need of a hot bath and fortunately,
the price included breakfast and bed tea, a nice local custom of
having tea served in your room at sunrise. The following day
we moved on to cheaper accommodations at a working girls
hostel for $1.75 total, which we could better afford.

We treated ourselves to a grand tour of the area, which
lasted from 9 to 6 and only cost us 75 cents each. The guide
took us to the second oldest cricket venue in India where we
watched part of a match – an endless competition with the
most complicated rules I have ever tried to understand. We
only watched part of the match because an entire one, we
learned, lasts for several days!

We moved on to admire the Raj Ghat, a black marble
platform and memorial where they cremated Mahatma
Gandhi. After a lunch break we toured Jantar Mantar obser-
vatory that houses a rare collection of ancient astronomical
instruments. It demonstrates the remarkable skills of a
scholarly prince (named Sawai Jai Singh) in the eighteenth
century. The guide led us to the India Gate, Humayn's Tomb
and Qutab Mintar, the very impressive soaring tower of
victory built in 1193 after the defeat of Delhi's last Hindu
Kingdom. It stands 240 feet tall, an amazing feat of construction for those times.

We also visited the largest mosque in the city, several Hindu
temples, and several other sites – all for 75 cents!

The next day we left for Agra by third class rail, but this
time it only took four hours. We stopped at a fort from which
we could see the famous Taj Majal in the distance. Even from
afar the site was awe-inspiring and something we had been
looking forward to for a long time. We made plans to visit
the memorial by moonlight, as we understood that was the
ultimate way to experience the remarkable ancient edifice.

My journal reads, *"That was the most fantastic, mystical place that I have ever seen, even though the moon was not full and would not be for a few more days."* The majestic white building appeared as if out of a dream with its domed roof and perfectly symmetrical architecture. When viewed from the base of the reflection pool, four tall white pillars stood like soldiers protecting their fortress.

We approached in a horse-drawn *tonga* and then walked up to the Taj Majal through a large entry gate. My first close-up view of the famous landmark was breathtaking. It was incredibly beautiful and massive – much larger that I had imagined. Moonlight softened the white marble, creating a breathtaking effect.

A guide took my arm and whisked me off to several side temples so that I could get different views of the main building. When I entered I discovered that they lighted the rooms with muted lanterns, highlighting the delicate marble inlay work. Precious gems were carefully inlaid in the beautiful marble. Standing inside I sensed a mystical image of the Maharani for whom they built this magnificent structure.

We saw cenotaphs or empty tombs that are monuments to Shah Jahan and his wife. We were permitted to touch the soft, cool marble of the vaults. Strolling through the pristine gardens, I remarked that it was truly the most impressive monument I had ever seen.

The Taj was a tribute from the Shah to his beloved wife and had taken 20,000 workers per day 22 years to build. Each worker had his hands cut off when his job ended so that he could never duplicate this magnificent structure, one of the seven wonders of the ancient world.

The next morning we came upon a snake charmer playing a recorder, (a type of flute) as his cobra rose out of its basket and opened its hood. I could not help but think that it was a sad looking reptile and an unimpressive show. Since we could only pay the bare minimum, the show was brief, but at least we were pleased to see the real thing and be able to describe how strange it was to our friends back home.

We boarded a local bus for Fatepur Sikri, a deserted city built by Akbar in the Sixteenth Century. They lived in that city for only 12 years when the water supply ran out and the population abandoned the site. It was remarkable because the city was still intact after all these hundreds of years. I tried to understand how the soft sandstone had lasted in such intense heat. They explained that the palace had its own form of air conditioning – a running water-cooling system that ran throughout the palace – and that the dry desert air aided in the preservation.

We headed back to the RR station for another grueling third class journey. All we could find to eat were peanuts and tangerines (things that could be peeled or shelled and the only safe food available on the train platform) before setting off on another arduous, uncomfortable train trip to our next Indian city.

CHAPTER TWENTY NINE
Benares, India
February 19, 1959

We spent a night draped over seats and suitcases in a third class train carriage, traveling 200 miles southeast to the city of Benares that lay on the banks of the Ganges River. We had a hard time sleeping on the hard wooden benches with the constant dust and dirt seeping in through open windows.

"I am very tired of being nice to all sorts of people," I muttered grumpily. "I feel like I did after a few months at the Expo, weary and just wanting to be left alone to fend for myself. But I can't do that – it would cost too much!"

We met a rather pushy man on the train named Mr. Saxena who was coming to Benares for the All-India Maha Sabha Party Congress. He insisted that we stay with him when we reached the city. He showed us his place, which was only one room and had no beds, so we carefully thanked him and looked for other accommodations. A man in the tourist office offered to let us stay in a spare room in the building. Once again, there were no beds, only a concrete floor covered by a threadbare rug. We decided to take him up on it as it was free and we could use our sleeping bags. The bathroom facility was the usual hole in the ground. There was no door to the room where we slept, so assorted people wandered in and out at will.

Looking down from our balcony that evening we could see 18 sacred cows and sundry dogs, cats and bulls gathered in the street below for their evening meal of garbage and hay. An Indian woman, sack in hand, stood waiting for the inevitable fresh dung. She would carefully select choice bits, pat it into shape and drop it into a bag. Later it would be dried and sold for fuel. Sue and I decided that if we got up by 4 a.m. we might get the "drop" on the other women and gather three bags full before breakfast. We agreed that the call letters for the All India radio station should be D-U-N-G.

Everywhere we went masses of people besieged us and so we hired a boat to take us out on the Ganges River in order to escape the crowds. The whole situation was beginning to get to us – the crowds pressing close, the heat and the squalid conditions. The city was the filthiest and the most primitive one I had ever seen.

It was very, very hot and we could see people (mostly men in loincloths) bathing in the river or just sitting around. The stench worsened as we walked through the crowded streets. Even the food smells were repulsive: the unfamiliar spices and strange food combinations made our stomachs turn.

They told us that the river was holy and very clean. "That's a laugh," I commented looking down at the floating debris. We saw many Ghats or steps leading down to the holy river which was a murky, unwelcoming brown color – anything but clean.

They were cremating bodies on the Ghats as we sailed by. We counted seven fires ablaze. One of the shrouds covering a body failed to extend to the exposed feet. Three bodies rested upon the pyre and two more awaited burning on the steps.

They bathed the bodies in the river and then wrapped them in a cheesecloth material, white for men, colors for women. We learned that they cremate the dead as soon as possible after their demise, in a matter of hours or as soon as they can find the most important family member who can light the match. After the boat ride we went to one of the best hotels in town for a meal because we had not eaten since breakfast the previous day and our stomachs were growling. At this point we needed to eat safe food in sanitary conditions. We walked through the crowded bazaar and it reminded me of a movie set or a contrived area put together for tourists. However, we had not seen a single tourist.

Merchants were hawking their wares and practically forcing items into our hands. The chaotic scene grew even worse as the word spread that Americans had arrived; the locals expected that we would be rich buyers. When we ambled through the streets, crowds pushed in around us. By the time we got back to our room there were 25 people trailing close behind. Perhaps Stew's latest outfit – consisting of lederhosen and a baggy brown sweater topped by three multi-colored scarves and the usual pith helmet – partly explained the attraction.

We decided to rent bicycles the following day in another attempt to escape the throngs. The day was beautiful: the sun shone brightly and the dry heat was bearable. The man at the tourist office told us that it was not possible to rent bikes, but Stewart forged ahead and found a deal that we could afford. You could bargain for almost anything in that city if you had the courage. While Stew bargained, about 150 people gathered around us staring and crowding so close that they were actually leaning into our bodies.

We set out through streets with barely enough space to maneuver between the rickshaws, holy cows and beggars. We picked our way past skinny women nursing babies as they raised their supplicating hands up crying out "*memsahib*" with pleading expressions on their faces.

We bicycled five miles to a small town called Sarnath. Peddling along over flat terrain, we admired a variety of beautiful tropical plants. We got off the bikes and walked through the streets, visiting the ruins of an ancient Hindu city as well as several Chinese Buddhist Temples.

After we rested in the soothing warm sun, we bicycled back to Benares with renewed spirits, having had a little respite from the crowds. We waited while Sue went into the post office and were amazed when more than 200 people gathered around us in a short five minutes. The police tried to break up the mob but the people paid no attention. We walked further but more people pushed and shoved us around. In that part of the world they had no regard for personal space.

Since we were not leaving until seven that evening, we decided to rent a junk to sail out on the river. Once again, our primary motivation was to avoid the crowds. The junk and driver cost fifty cents for four hours and took us out into the middle of the river where we swam in our underwear and were completely refreshed. At last, we had found clean water!

CHAPTER THIRTY
Calcutta, India
February 23, 1959

We boarded a railroad workers' car for the next leg and were relieved to find it was much more comfortable than the previous one. Our entire railroad trip across India had cost a total of $8 each. No wonder it was a nightmare of discomfort! What did we expect for that amount of money?

We played bridge until 2 a.m. and then tried to sleep on the hard benches. Daylight dawned revealing a drastic change in scenery. We were now steaming along through thick vegetation abundant with lush tropical plants. Through clearings along the tracks, we could see thick forests in the distance. The area became tropical; we saw huts with thatched roofs scattered throughout the landscape.

We arrived in Calcutta at 10 the next morning and found a room where we five could stay for 12 rupees, or about $12 per night. (Stewart was continuing to accompany us for the rest of the trip). My first impression of Calcutta was that of a much

more Asian city. Men pulled rickshaws through the streets in
this hotter and more humid climate. I felt that we were again
entering a new phase of the journey; this was our introduction
to the Far East.

Gloria and I went to the offices of Mackenzie and
Mackinnon to try to recover our deposit for the Basrah boat
booking. We found the people to be very nice but they told
us that they needed a letter of authorization from the Reserve
Bank in order to refund our money in rupees, the Indian
currency. Another authorization would enable us to change
the rupees into pounds sterling...but they could never convert
it into U.S. dollars. They had been working on this project for
some time but warned that it would take still longer as business
transactions were typically very slow in Calcutta.

We went to the Reserve Bank ourselves to help speed up
the process, but when we arrived at 2:45, we learned that the
bank had closed 15 minutes earlier. Once again our attempt
to get our refund was foiled and the Iraqi portion of our plans
continued to dog us.

We walked through Calcutta's beautiful Victoria Memorial, a
lovely display of tropical trees and flowers. They labeled them
with their botanical and common name and noted their natural
origin, much to my delight, as I have always been interested in
horticulture. This was a most fantastic day; I felt very happy
and was becoming increasingly fond of Calcutta. I was
finding it to be a much more welcoming and interesting city
than New Delhi.

Gloria and I returned to the Reserve Bank the next day
and ran into more delays. The bankers agreed to write the
authorization letter only if we prepared a full description of
our transaction: an explanation of why we had not taken the
boat, as well as identifying the transportation we had taken in
its place and why and where we had done so. They told us to
come back later, which we did, but when we returned they had
still not written the letter.

We never got our money back despite so much persistent effort on our part. Travel arrangements were not as sophisticated in those days. It was very difficult to deal with so many transactions in countries that operated in diverse ways. Even our endless patience did not pay off in the end.

We went to the zoo that afternoon to take our minds off our misery and met a friendly little man who happily told us the name of every single animal on his guided tour. We rode an elephant: an experience you would not wish to have if you tended to suffer from seasickness. First, we climbed a tall ladder to reach the seat atop the immense animal. Then we rode around feeling as though we were back on the ship heading for Brussels in a turbulent sea. Still, it was another unique experience and one I would talk about for years.

The zoo staff invited us into the office of the volunteer director of the board, a very intelligent man who had attended MIT. He had a thriving metal business in Calcutta which required him to fly to the U.S. about five times each year. We enjoyed a wonderful conversation with him and were surprised to hear him opine that he felt the best action for the U.S. would be to cut off all aid to India. He suggested that we should have a trade agreement that would make his country work for it.

The following day we went to the airline office (Cathay Pacific Airways) to request a student reduction. They gave us a 15% discount on a booking through to Hong Kong, including a side trip to Singapore and Indonesia, at a cost of $230 each. I considered this a good deal and one that would assure us of a timely arrival in Hong Kong and Yokahama, Japan from where we would board a ship to sail across the Pacific and home.

A snake charmer in Agra, India

pp.152
Above: Stewart riding an elephant in India

*Below: The four of us and fellow travelers
watching a Balinese dancer perform*

Above: Boarding the plane in Calcutta top to bottom: Gloria, Jane, Sue, me and Stewart

Left: Stewart and Indonesian friend in Jakarta

CHAPTER THIRTY ONE
At Home in a Brothel
Bangkok, Thailand

February 26, 1959

Our departure from India marked a new phase in our mode
of travel. Until this time we had employed at least 10 different
kinds of transportation: car, ship, taxi, bicycle rickshaw, human
rickshaw, bus, horse-drawn *tonga*, 3rd class airplane, varieties
of low train classes and even an elephant in the Calcutta Zoo.
The discount from CPA (Cathay Pacific Airlines) made it possible
for us to travel "in style" for the first time.

   We donned whatever finery we still had – decent cotton
dresses and stylish 3-inch high heels – and proudly climbed
the stairs to the waiting plane. We loaded our arms with excess
baggage and held our heads high. Only Stewart chose to retain
his habitual attire of lederhosen and pith helmet, which caused
some fellow passengers to remark that he must be the original
"ugly American."

Like excited children, we greedily consumed one and then a second cocktail offered by the steward. The chicken dinner that followed seemed like a meal fit for the gods when compared to our customary Indian train meals of oranges, peanuts, bananas and tea…or just plain bread for Jane, who refused to taste any of the ethnic food in these countries. In fact, she had bought an ample supply of K rations at the PX in Brussels to carry her through the automobile portion of our journey.

We were in high spirits at the end of our meal when we led several hearty choruses of "On the Road to Mandalay" as we circled the Rangoon Airport preparing to land.

From my distant view, I could see that it was a more modern city than I had imagined. For some strange reason I had always heard of Rangoon and imagined it to be the most foreign and exotic place in the world. Colonial Yangon, its original name, boasted of spacious parks and lakes as well as a mix of traditional wooden temples, famous pagodas with upturned rooflines and modern buildings. The former British Colony established its independence in 1948 and is now known as Myanmar.

I had long dreamed of visiting Rangoon and at least I had the chance to glimpse it… albeit for only a very short time. When we took off, I could see the lighted temples of that magical land.

A brothel in Bangkok became our next home away from home. Within all the reaches of our combined imaginations, we had not seen that one coming!

The airline steward, Joe Tao, distributed customs forms on which we were required to state our residence while in Thailand before landing. He had befriended us during the flight and understood that we were traveling on a shoestring and had not made advance reservations for our lodging. He suggested that we list the Hotel Trocadero for the time being and offered to help us find accommodations when we arrived.

A blast of stifling, hot, humid air and a thousand mosquitoes greeted us as we deplaned. We looked at each other in surprise, and tried to laugh it off. We passed through customs and were loaded onto an airline bus that took us into the city.

A 20-mile ride, stopping at several elegant hotels to drop off passengers, took us to our destination in town. The brightly lit city looked exciting: we were launching into a completely new part of the world and were all enthusiastic and anxious for a new adventure.

We arrived at the Trocadero Hotel at 1 a.m. and roused the night clerk who said that he could put us up for $3 a night each. This price was way beyond our budget so we sleepily sat in the lobby and waited for our friend Joe Tao to come and help us when he finished his airline duties. He said he knew of less expensive accommodations and beckoned to Gloria and me to follow him out of the lobby, around the corner and into an alleyway.

We entered the side of a building thru a dingy doorway and climbed two flights of stairs. Our suspicions became aroused when we walked down a long barren hallway. Joe motioned for us to wait while he entered a room at the far end of the building. Small lizards crawled up and down the walls and thousands of mosquitoes swarmed around as we stood in the dimly lit passageway. We assumed that all the guests were asleep at such a late hour.

Joe reappeared with his friend, a slight young Thai gentleman who led us up another flight of stairs and down a corridor where we passed doors that were slightly ajar. We could not help but steal a few glances and were surprised to see that all the rooms were filled with empty liquor bottles and beds with mussed sheets. Joe's friend showed us one clean room with two double beds and another with a sofa bed. He said we could have this and another room (for Stewart) for a total of $5 a night.

We went back to the Trocadero, collected our luggage and our travelling mates and happily settled in for the night in our usual state of exhaustion. We were awakened intermittently by the twittering of small voices and footsteps pattering along the hallway at all hours…that led us to conclude that this was not your ordinary hotel. It suddenly became clear that we were in a house of ill repute!

In view of this rather unsettling observation, we all agreed that we would be perfectly safe as long as we all stuck together and kept the door locked. We made a pact that we would not leave the room alone, even for trips to the bathroom. Returning to our beds, we had managed to reassure ourselves enough to get a full night's sleep.

The next morning we ventured down the front staircase and found a nightclub/snack bar on the ground floor with windows facing out onto the main street, around the corner from our shady entryway of the night before. We wolfed down a full American-style breakfast of eggs, bacon and even milk, all for 75 cents. The owner came up to our table and enthusiastically explained that his son was studying in the U.S. and that he was very happy to be able to help travelling students, especially Americans. Once again, we were experiencing acts of kindness and hospitality in a most unusual place! Our host not only served good food at the snack bar, but apparently had a thriving business upstairs!

Bangkok took on a completely new appearance by the light of day. Compared to hot and dusty India, it was a land of vibrant color and a land of plenty. The exuberant hues of the lively markets displaying lush tropical flowers and fruits, the splashing colors of the enchanting temples and even the bright orange of the Buddhist monks' robes brought us alive and made us receptive to the warm smiles of the friendly Thai people. The humid tropical climate made twice-daily showers a necessity but hardly diminished our enthusiasm for this ancient Kingdom of Siam.

We returned to our rooms and learned that the owner of the establishment had invited us to join him in the nightclub downstairs that evening. I had just received a letter from Ann

Coco of Baton Rouge, Louisiana – a perceptive young woman who had become a good pal of mine at the Fair. She generously included a check for $10 saying that I would probably be in need of a square meal by this time and to have one on her!

We splurged and spent the whole $10 savoring delicious Thai food at a table right next to the dance floor; they even left off the service charge on our bill. The food was a real adventure since none of us had ever eaten the tasty and spicy dishes they presented. Thai food was almost unknown in The United States at that time, but has earned its way to becoming a very popular cuisine.

The following day Gloria and Sue contacted their friend Mr. Binich Sampatisiri who had been commissioner general of the Thai Pavilion in Brussels. He invited us to his home for dinner and planned to send a car to pick us up that evening. We did not dare admit that we were staying in a brothel, so we told him that we were at the Trocadero. When the appointed hour came, we quickly dressed and ran over to the Trocadero lobby where we sat innocently on lush couches awaiting his arrival.

Mr. Sampatisiri had arranged for us to have a tour of the city the next day that began with a visit to a museum featuring Thai history and customs. A prince, the nephew of the former king, guided us and carefully described details of his culture and customs. His description evoked memories of the play (and movie) "Anna and the King of Siam."

Continuing the tour, we found that the entire city was a myriad of bright reds, oranges and yellows enhanced by glistening gold touches. Brightly decorated Buddhist temples seemed gaudy to our conservative tastes.

We even visited the Pasteur Institute, a snake farm where they milked cobra, king cobra and krait to produce serum to treat snakebites. I became very uneasy when they took the snakes out of their cages to demonstrate the milking process.

Joe Tao arranged for another memorable tour which started with an early morning boat ride through the great *kongs*
(canals) of Bangkok where we saw goods being bought and
sold from little sampans which constituted a floating market.
Smiling children greeted us happily as they took their morning
baths in the canal, which bordered on a jungle abounding in
tropical ferns and palms. We noticed small subsidiary waterways which we wanted to explore but could not enter because
our boat was too large.

We climbed to the Temple of the Dawn by way of a staircase that led straight up the steepest and most narrow steps I
had ever ascended. The dizzying view from the top revealed
the entire city of Bangkok. In the distance we saw the royal
boathouse that stored brightly decorated ceremonial barges
which were used for funerals and coronations and measured
a full city block in length.

Although Bangkok had become modern, 100 healthy
specimens of manhood towed these long barges through the
canal by walking along the shore with towropes over their
broad shoulders.

We walked back into the jungle to visit a fishing village
by moonlight. We crossed over a wooden plank leading to
thatched houses that perched atop high stilts. The roofs of
the homes curved upward to frighten away evil spirits. This
ingenious design makes them cooler in summer, drier in the
rainy season and protects the residents from deadly snakes.
Below the huts, we saw pigs eating garbage and chickens
picking at a muddy surface. The residents all peeked out from
their homes with bright smiles and welcoming waves.

We travelled by city bus to visit the temple of the reclining
Buddha, a huge gaudy figure covered with gold paint. We
made our own pencil rubbings on rice paper from the carvings
on the outer walls. I still treasure those black and white
rubbings that hang on the wall in my dining room.

CHAPTER THIRTY TWO
Kuala Lumpur, Malaysia
March 2, 1959

After the delightful three-day visit in Bangkok, we flew south
to Malaysia, descending over lush green hills and dense jungle
before landing at the modern looking Kuala Lumpur airport.
The plane's crew ushered us into a waiting room while the
authorities checked our passports.

I approached a cute Malaysian airhostess named Norbetia
and asked if she might know of a cheap place where we could
stay. She generously suggested that we could share her quarters
and escorted us to a Malaysian Air Lines Volkswagen bus that
drove us to the apartment that she shared with three other girls.

The first roommate we met was Norbetia's sister Nobia,
a tiny person with short, black, wavy hair and a happy face.
Next, we met the other two roommates: Siti, another beautiful,
tiny lady who had shiny black hair that fell to her waist, and
Rosalie, a slender Chinese girl who appeared to be the humorist

of the group. Rosalie said that Sue and I could stay in the home of her boyfriend Bill, as there was not room for all of us in this small space.

Mr. Harris, a talkative, amusing Englishman came to the front door and promptly offered to have Stewart stay with him. Our struggles seemed to be ending as we entered this friendly, welcoming world of the Far East where complete strangers were offering free accommodations.

Our hosts took us out for the evening to an "amusement park" – the major nighttime attraction for young people in Kuala Lumpur. The amusement parks were unlike those in our country; instead, they are nightspots and bars that provide various types of entertainment. Our first stop was a large café where we had drinks and watched young Malaysian women lining up on a stage prepared for "taxi dancing." They hire these women to dance with customers on a dance-by-dance basis. Men purchased tickets for 10 cents apiece for an opportunity to move around the dance floor, never touching, but talking. We wondered if this was leading to a more involved and intimate evening, but were afraid to ask.

We entered a theater featuring Chinese opera in which one single performance lasts for three days. Meanwhile the audience is free to wander in and out as they wish. The heavily made-up actors wore elaborate costumes. Their voices sounded like high-pitched screeching and it was hard to imagine that this was their idea of singing. We were not able to understand the language or meaning of this lengthy performance but it clearly had great entertainment value for the locals.

Our hostesses had an unusual lifestyle since Malaysian young women of their class seldom lived away from their families. Traditionalists looked down upon them for their adopted western ways. Norbetia, Nobia and Siti were related to the royal family and therefore were considered upper class.

Rosalie was the divorced mother of two children. She explained that since she lived in a Muslim country, her husband had only to say "I divorce you" three times and the separation was official. He automatically had custody of the children and she was left to fend for herself. She did not tell us how she felt about this situation but she seemed perfectly at ease with her present life.

Sue and I happily settled into Bill's apartment, which was open to the outside and had no screens or glass on the windows. Tiny lizards fascinated us as they crawled over the white walls with their suction cupped feet. The apartment was a luxurious respite which we had not anticipated. We shared a large and well-decorated bedroom, which was an all too rare pleasure during our travels. When we awoke the following morning Sue told me that she had discovered a very cute little *amah* (house-keeper) in the kitchen who said, "Good morning missy" as she prepared our breakfast. It was such a treat to have someone so kindly welcome and pamper us for a change!

Our friends drove us far into the jungle that afternoon. We walked along a path through deep snake grass to a beautiful waterfall surrounded by wild orchids. We donned sarongs which Nobetia had graciously loaned us and stepped into the cooling, soothing shower – recovering from the shock of having suddenly entered a land of tropical heat and humidity. The sarongs tended to slip a bit but we managed them quite well for novices.

Our 12 new friends were at the airport to give us a proper send off the following day. A reporter interviewed and photo-graphed our group for an article, which appeared in the Straits Times, indicating that we were four American travelers accom-panied by a dance partner and cigarette lighter (Stewart).

Once again we had enjoyed an amazing experience, completely unplanned and unexpected in its spontaneous hospitality and friendship.

CHAPTER THIRTY THREE
Singapore
March 3, 1959

Singapore is the most beautiful, clean and pristine city that I have ever seen. My journal entry read, *"I have never been as excited as I am to be here. We are going to stay at the world famous Raffles Hotel and have reached the half-way point of our trip."*

Jane's father had decided to treat us to one night at the prestigious hotel to help transition our "culture shock." We entered our large, elegantly furnished room and wondered if we were in heaven. The four of us ran around in circles like crazy people. We were so excited to be in such a luxurious setting that we immediately phoned room service to order drinks...and almost forgot to ask the price first.

Mr. Soong, the same sympathetic airline steward whom we had met on our first flight from Calcutta, befriended us. It was more common in the Far East to have stewards rather than female flight attendants on the plane crew. He invited us to join him and his friends for a tour of the city that evening. We were delighted to accept this invitation and explore the new city with enthusiasm.

Gloria had become friends with a countess while working at the Fair. This gracious lady put us in touch with her daughter, a resident of Singapore, who was anxious to welcome us to her city. When Gloria phoned, the countess' daughter immediately sent her husband over to greet us. This well dressed, proper gentleman explained that they were not able to entertain us that evening, however they had made plans for the rest of our visit.

We asked for suggestions from the hotel door attendant who steered us to an affordable restaurant down the street where we dined on familiar simple hamburgers at a sidewalk café. After dinner, Mr. Soong guided us to the local amusement park, again a popular nightspot for young people. We later enjoyed drinks on a moonlit rooftop terrace overlooking the city.

The next morning we ordered breakfast in the room before setting out on our errands. We transacted business at the offices of American Express, the U.S.I.S (U.S. Information Service) and the American President Lines, where we secured passage from Japan to San Francisco for the final leg of our journey. Stewart secured cheap deck space on a Dutch ship to Indonesia, but the ship refused us passage because we were Caucasian women. And so our quirky comrade journeyed separately to Jakarta where we saw him briefly...but our paths did not cross again until he rejoined us on the deck of the President Wilson in Yokohama, Japan, for our voyage home.

We returned to the Raffles and the countess' daughter picked us up and took us to her beautiful modern home in the hills, where we stayed for the rest of our visit. We lunched, swam and enjoyed a relaxing afternoon at her elegant country club. That evening our hosts took us to the Chinese district for an authentic Szechwan meal.

Chinese works of art and colorful lanterns decorated the large restaurant. The food was delicious and far different from the ordinary Chinese restaurant food that they served at home. After dinner, we walked through the city and passed apartments where as many as 25 people resided in one unit. The crowded conditions did not appear to be a problem as they waved and peered at us with curious smiling faces.

We came upon a funeral procession marching slowly along the street, setting paper icons on fire to float up into the night sky and escort the body into the afterworld. They burned pictures of paper houses, cars and money to accompany the deceased and lighten his or her burden in heaven.

The rest of our stay in Singapore was wonderful. We were able to rest in the lap of luxury. Our gracious hosts did everything for us: Madame even made dresses for us out of cool, light cotton material so that we would be comfortable for the rest of our travels in the hot and muggy country of Indonesia. We had not been able to pack warm weather clothing in our limited luggage space. The countess' daughter spoke French and enjoyed the added bonus of speaking her native language during our stay.

Jane had promised to take a turkey to her family in Indonesia, our next destination. After much research, we found a market where she could purchase the fowl that was such a treat to all Americans – but a rarity in the rest of the world. We arranged to have it stored in the airport restaurant refrigerator overnight before our departure. While we were strolling along the streets of Singapore in search of a market, Jane found a stray cat that she insisted upon rescuing. We almost missed our plane to Jakarta the next morning because we had to take time to deliver the animal to the local S.P.C.A. on our way to the airport. Jane was an inveterate animal lover and could not be dissuaded, even at the risk of missing a flight. How could we not love her for that?

CHAPTER THIRTY FOUR
Jakarta, Indonesia
March 10, 1959

We left Singapore and headed for Jakarta, where we would
unofficially mark our half way around the world destination
on March 10, 1959. During the Garuda Airways flight to Jakarta,
Jane was so excited at the thought of seeing her parents
again that she nearly parachuted from the plane while it circled
the airfield.

Our flight was taking us low over hundreds of small, lush,
green islands scattered in a clear emerald sea. We skimmed
above the surface of the water and ran into turbulence that
made us fearful that we would not survive this leg of our long
journey. The small plane held only a few passengers seated in
the fuselage below the wing structure, an airplane configuration
that we had not previously experienced. However, the awesome
scenery helped to distract us.

We were overwhelmed when the cabin door opened and the hot, humid air blasted in our faces. We spotted Jane's family waiting on the tarmac. The first question we asked was "Do you have a toilet seat?" The reply astounded us: "two." Her father, a college professor, went to work in Indonesia to help guide the country in its growing educational challenges. They were living in Bandung, an enclave in the mountainous area of Java and home of the university. While in Jakarta we had a brief rendezvous with our friend Don Summerville, who would be flying out an hour after our arrival.

We checked in at the U.S. Embassy where Jane found a note from Stewart who had taken a slow boat to Indonesia earlier. He wrote that he was living in a low cost hotel in town. A young Indonesian woman was looking after him. He said he would meet us in Bandung later. If we wished to contact him, we could call the hotel and ask for his friend (whose name he mentioned). As it turned out Stewart did not join us in Bandung, in fact we only saw him briefly in Jakarta with his young woman in tow and not again until we boarded the ship in Japan. He was a free spirit and probably needed to be on his own for a while.

We set out for Bandung, a four-hour trip by car through the most beautiful green countryside that I had ever seen. A multitude of different crops covered the many hills and mountains. It looked like almost anything would grow in this ideal climate. The streets were crowded with vendors selling pineapples, bananas and coconuts. They toted their wares on a carrying pole or a yoke that they balanced on both shoulders. The small thin men carried their burdensome weight gracefully. We drove past pristine rice paddies terraced into the verdant hillsides creating a most pleasing panorama.

We stopped at a restaurant atop the Puncak Pass for a delicious bowl of pea soup, a familiar and soothing meal in the cooler climate of the mountaintop. The scenery was breath-taking: miles and miles of lush greenery spread over hills and mountains like a velvet carpet. We passed through Bogar, a town that boasted of having the largest botanical garden in the world. It was also the site of the palace of Sukarno, who led Indonesia's struggle for independence from the Netherlands and served as its first President from 1945 to 1967. We arrived at the Bancroft's home in Bandung early that evening feeling exhausted and drained from the oppressive heat. We felt like we had finally come home. We even had room to unpack completely! Their complex was a welcoming sight with its many open-air rooms and patio leading to a refreshing swimming pool, which we took advantage of immediately. The following day we enjoyed a "divine" turkey dinner, thanks to Jane who had carried the fowl on her lap all the way from Singapore. I phoned home for the first time since I had left Brussels and was thrilled to hear my mother's voice and catch up on her news.

We spent six wonderful days with that most hospitable family and loved swimming in their pool, relaxing and having them take care of us for a change. At the end of the week, we learned that we must return to Jakarta to begin a student tour that would take us east to the island of Bali. Jane's father had arranged for us to join the excursion, conducted and paid for by the Indonesian Ministry of Education. He felt he was giving us a great opportunity to see and learn about Java and Bali, for which we were very grateful. However, when the going got rough and we were tempted to bail out, we knew we were obligated to see the trip to the end so that we would not disgrace this kind man.

CHAPTER THIRTY FIVE
At Home in Bandung
March 1959

Easter Sunday at the Bancroft home was a gay affair complete
with the traditional egg hunt, followed by church and a
celebratory dinner. With a mixture of anticipation and dread,
we looked forward to our two-week student tour of Java and
Bali that was to begin the next morning. We knew that the trip
would be rough and facilities would be primitive, but we were
eager to see and learn about this exotic country. Mrs. Bancroft
thoughtfully provided us with a stash of food and insect spray
in a yellow carrying case and Dr. Bancroft slipped in a bottle
of scotch for the tougher times.

   We left Bandung in the very early morning to return to the
blistering heat of Jakarta and the beginning of our arduous
student tour. We met with Miss Budearjon at the Ministry of
Education who outlined our program for the next few weeks.
We doubted that we could survive this rigorous schedule, as we

still felt overwhelmed by the intense heat and humidity. She collected our passports to extend our visas. Even though she was a trusted official, we hesitated to relinquish those documents that we had clung to so steadfastly for the last many months.

Miss Budearjon introduced us to four young students who would be our guides. Every question we asked they answered with a "yes." They were eager to please but did not necessarily understand the question. They led us to the "Wismarini" student girls' hostel where we were staying in Jakarta. We followed our guides down the street and into a tall white building where we climbed three flights of stairs only to discover that we were in the wrong place. We retraced our steps and climbed another three flights to our accommodations: two tiny rooms with narrow beds outfitted with bottom sheets and pillows only.

We were glad to have the chance to rest and recover from the exertion of climbing so many stairs in the oppressive heat. We were exhausted from the heat and humidity, both of which were in the 90s. We took advantage of the local custom of a short siesta before going to the dining hall to eat a tasty western style lunch. When asked if we liked rice and Indonesian food, we were too polite to answer honestly – and were therefore served nothing but rice three times a day for the remainder of our stay! All of the dishes were set out under individual cheesecloth mini tents to stave off the multitude of flying insects.

We took another siesta after lunch, hoping that our bodies would adjust to the weather conditions and relieve our exhaustion. The difference in temperature from Bandung to Jakarta was at least 10 degrees due to the change in altitude.

As the evening approached and the air cooled down, the students suggested that we go to the harbor cafe in their Volkswagen bus for a refreshing drink. We sat on the terrace and watched another beautiful sunset. Our guides

spoke Dutch fluently because it was their primary language
in school.

Two of the students were celebrating the month of Ramadan,
a time when all Muslims fast from sunrise to sunset for 29
days. They explained that they would eat a big meal at 7 p.m.
and another at 3 a.m. so that they could last through the day
without even a drink of water.

We visited the home of one of the girls who introduced
us to her seven brothers and sisters. This large family was
a typical one for that area. They had furnished their home
comfortably; her parents appeared to be well off. She drove us
through a residential area in the family Pontiac and pointed out
many modern houses and apartments that were a huge contrast
to the squalid buildings in other parts of the city.

When I returned to the U.S. friends asked me which was my
favorite city in the world. My answer was standard: "I can't
say, but I can tell you that Jakarta is the armpit of the world."
I came to this conclusion after we visited many museums,
markets, tourist sites and the aquarium. I found all of these
to be "...hotter than hell, smelly, and difficult to visit due to
impossible traffic jams. Open sewers ran down the sides of
the streets." I did note, however, that the aquarium displayed
the most beautiful and unique tropical fish that I had ever seen.

After each tour, we would return to the "bare bones" hostel
for another meal of cold rice.

Finally the heat and depression got the best of us. The
weather was so oppressive that we felt we could barely breathe.
The future seemed very grim as we were about to leave on a
two week trip with 30 Indonesian and Malaysian students.
We were already tired from our difficult and long journey to
Indonesia that had taken us through 26 countries.

I began to feel very uncomfortable in the guise of a student,
since I had reached the age of 25 by that time. I was having
trouble being pals with these young people, especially considering the maturity I had gained from being on my own for so

long. We tried to have conversations with them but they were not able to understand our English very well. The standard answer to every question was still "yes."

A professor at the university invited us to his home for a tasty authentic Indonesian meal. His daughter performed a folk dance in the costume of a Java dancer, telling the story of a prince and his love. We watched two couples dance a number from northern Sumatra. They asked us to perform so the other girls sang a few songs in three-part harmony while I mouthed the words. My pals had discovered what I had known since grammar school: when I sang I threw the whole group off!

The following morning we ate breakfast with a charming woman who interviewed us for the local newspaper. We later attended a lecture at the university given by a senator from the Philippines. He made us aware of how close the parallel was between his country and Indonesia. For instance, he explained, the two countries produced 70% of the coconut crop in the world and yet the market price was set in London, San Francisco and New York instead of in their part of the world. He was attempting to right this situation.

The Ministry invited us and the other students to attend a performance one evening at the Christian Students' Association. The show was set to begin at 7 p.m…. but when we arrived they announced that there would be a delay because the stage-hands who had been fasting all day had gone out for a meal. The show finally began at 9 p.m. after we had been sitting in our chairs fighting off bugs for two hours.

The performance included several kinds of dances, recitations, vocal solos and piano numbers…and a guitar group known as the "Blue Boys" offering their rendition of American Rock and Roll. The first two dancers from northern Sumatra performed well enough but the show that followed was hard to take seriously. The "Blue Boys" took stage dressed in shiny blue satin shirts and black pegged pants singing several Elvis Presley numbers.

The next act was a poor imitation of the Ink Spots and then of Harry Belafonte. Next, a local man sang, accompanied by his very large Dutch wife on piano. Even I described his voice as "tragic." The audience hissed, booed and guffawed as he sang on. A slouching character appeared on stage and tripped over his feet as he bowed to the audience. He began to play a minuet, hesitated, and started over again. We thought it was an amusing comedy act until we found out that the poor soul was serious.

The next day Teppi, Dr. Bancroft's driver, took us back to the Ministry of Education to retrieve our passports. This turned out to be another confusing situation because they told us that the office was closed despite the fact that we had made an appointment with Miss Budearjon at 8:15 a.m. Teppi took us around to the back of the building where attendants insisted that we fill out forms before entering. We forced our way past them and found her office where she at her desk waiting for us. Apparently, communication was not their forte.

Our passports had not yet been processed so she asked us to return at 2 that afternoon. She had prepared a letter for Garuda Airlines assuring them that we qualified for a student discount. Garuda would not give us the discount because we were not residents of Singapore where we had made our application. We continued to go round and round in circles and finally agreed to have our passports forwarded to Bandung – hoping against all odds that the mail would be reliable.

When we returned to Bandung we learned that we had already missed one appointment with the student group. They had made plans for us for every minute of every day up until our departure. I said, "I am not sure that I am going to be able to live through this."

We travelled by train for the first part of our journey from Bandung to Jogjakarta, Surabaya and Malang. An entire book could be written about Indonesian trains, but suffice to say that they are extremely overcrowded and the air conditioning in first and second class (where the windows are, incidentally, sealed shut) works intermittently or not at all. The resultant pressure cooker effect turns even a well-tanned hide into a pale face at the end of six or eight hours.

Those five days were the most difficult of our entire trip. We left Bandung Monday morning at 9 and boarded a third class train accompanied by three student guides. It was hotter and more humid than it was in India and the passenger car was completely overcrowded. Passengers were crouching all over the floor. I read one whole book during the journey; it was the only way I could find distraction from the miserable conditions. I wrote this gloomy observation in my journal:

"I am suffering a new ailment, my feet and ankles are horribly swollen and I am sure that I am falling apart for good."

The locomotive looked like something out of an old western movie. A flatcar loaded with armed military to guard against bandits followed the locomotive.

We arrived in Jogjakarta at about seven that evening covered in dust and dirt and checked into another youth hostel.

Jogjakarta is the capital city of the Jogjakarta region of Java, the largest island in the Indonesian archipelago. It is renowned as a center of classical Javanese fine art and culture such as batik, ballet, drama, music, poetry and puppet shows...an important part of Indonesian culture.

Our accommodations were the usual – two small connecting rooms with beds, bottom sheets and a washing room for dip baths. The toilet facilities were smelly, alive with large cockroaches and equipped with a bucket for flushing. We had brought our standard bottle of cheap perfume, which we poured on a handkerchief or rag and held over our noses so that we could survive the smell. To this day I have nightmares about searching for a clean bathroom...and suddenly awaken in the night to find that I really need to get up and go.

After another breakfast of cold rice and tea, we boarded another train. We were very excited because they told us that we had second-class tickets in an air-conditioned car. We soon found that the air conditioning did not work and the windows would not open. The temperature reached 105 as I sat in a pool of sweat trying to keep up with mopping the sweat dripping from my body.

When we arrived in Surabaya that afternoon, I had a raging headache and my feet and ankles were swelling. Surabaya is Indonesia's second largest city and the capital of the province of East Java. It is the birthplace of President Sukarno.

Throughout our trip the thoughtful and accommodating Indonesian students tried their best to keep us happy. When we got to Malang, our next port of call, we joined up with a group of Malayan students. We left the train and continued in a small bus that lacked comfortable seats but stood up amazingly well over miles and miles of kidney-rupturing roads.

The scenery was incredible. We never ceased to exclaim over the lush tropical vegetation, the stately palms, the misty blue volcanic mountains and the neatly terraced rice fields. Unfortunately the lovely rice that we saw growing inevitably found its way to our table. Three times a day we stared at the cold, white mound set before us and decided that the crackers and peanut butter so graciously provided by Mrs. Bancroft would make a tasty alternative.

We used the insect spray but it was no match for some of the heartier varieties of cockroaches and spiders we encountered. The favorite hangout of the cockroaches was the bath, where they would merrily play hide and seek while we attempted to wash off layers of dust with dippers of cold water and soap.

CHAPTER THIRTY SIX
Eastern Java
April 1959

I can best describe our trip through eastern Java to Bali by quoting my journal, *"This is a most fantastic place! I wish I were not so tired so that I might enjoy it more. I have just witnessed some of the most beautiful scenery in the world."* We passed acres of magnificently terraced green rice paddies spilling over the sides of hills. We travelled alongside the loveliest seacoast in the world where the clear blue water crashes onto pristine white sand beaches. Tropical coconut groves offer the backdrop for this peaceful setting.

I still had a raging headache. We traveled for one and a half hours to Malang, which had been a popular destination for European residents during the time of Dutch colonization. The city was famous for its cool air, but we could not seem to find any. We visited the university and went to the home of some Americans who were living and working there. I found the evening to be most disappointing as they and their friends only talked about what they could buy cheap and what was wrong with the local people. I realized what the term "ugly Americans" describes.

The next morning we got up again at 5, and boarded two buses. One was large and "ratty" and the other was a smaller version of the same thing. Gloria and I climbed into the smaller one and sat next to a boy who drilled me for two hours: "How much does your father earn? Who is paying for your trip," – questions that I considered nosey and inappropriate. We made only one stop to take in the beautiful view.

I was seriously worried, thinking, "I do not see how I can live through two more weeks of these conditions." We stopped for lunch and ate the sandwiches that our American friends had prepared while the other students ate rice in a small, dirty café.

Our final stop in Java was the city of Banyuwangi at the eastern most tip of the island. All 34 of us checked into a rundown hotel with only four bathrooms. Several of those rooms did not have water, only broken faucets. Mosquito netting draped over our small cots, a welcome relief from the thousands of bugs that were always buzzing around. We went to the governor's home for a typical rice dinner and returned to our hotel for an early bedtime; we had to be up again at five the next morning.

After another rice breakfast at the governor's home, they bused us to the ferry that would take us 90 miles across the water to the tropical paradise of Bali. The "ferry" turned out to be a broken down work boat which we boarded by walking up a narrow plank from the sandy beach.

We stood on the deck of the ferry during the entire trip and finally spotted the beautiful volcanic black sand beaches of Bali.

We landed by running aground on the beach of the enchanting island in the pouring rain. Few tourists had discovered this idyllic place in 1959 and so there were few accommodations available. We, of course headed for the first youth hostel.

After a two hour wait in the hot sun we boarded buses to Denpasar, the capital city, which is on the southeastern tip of the island. It is the most populated city on the island. Because it is not near the volcano, it has beautiful white sand beaches.

We bounced over roads full of potholes and bumps. We saw roaring, rushing streams flowing out of the hills, emptying their muddy waters into the sea. Only a few of the women were wearing tops. They had passed a law requiring that women cover the top half of their bodies but most of the older set refused to comply.

We arrived at a newly built hostel and were greeted by a small old man dressed in a batik wraparound from his waist to his ankles, batik cap, and striped top. We ate our usual rice dinner and went to bed early so we would be ready for whatever tomorrow would bring.

We visited the Elephant Cave, a Hindu holy place of the 10th and 11th centuries that they had excavated in 1952. The government was required to provide public bathing places for the population and had developed an amazing system of underground canals that kept the baths filled with water.

We stopped at Tampaksiring, a town in central Bali dating back to the 10th century where Sukarno built his presidential palace. We walked along a ravine and crossed a very shaky bamboo bridge that spanned a holy river. There were large tombs carved from the volcanic rock in the hillside. They believed they were the tombs of an ancient king and his wives, surrounded by waterfalls spewing out of lush green hills. We visited the Tirta Empul temple that is famous for the holy water in which the Balinese people bathe for purification.

CHAPTER THIRTY-SEVEN

The Monkey Dance
April 4, 1959

One evening we travelled by bus to a small village deep in the jungle to attend a performance of the famous Monkey Dance. Our trip included about six stops for bus repairs before we crossed another very rickety bridge. They asked the boys to get out and walk across separately because the bridge was not strong enough to support the entire weight. That pronouncement made us girls wonder if we would make it.

When we finally reached our destination, we saw a clearing with straw mats around a large candelabrum. In a large circle around the mats were rows of chairs and benches for the audience. One hundred and twenty men sat cross-legged on the mats, bare to the waist with black and white checked cloths tied around their waists. Each man had placed red flowers behind both ears.

The men began to chant, providing a background for the entire hour-long performance. The chanting mimicked a chorus of monkeys in varying degrees of excitement. The exotic show became very emotional as girls came on stage from time to time, rocking back and forth and waving their outstretched arms. This dance, the Ketchak or Dance of the Bone, told of a girl put in a trance so that she could communicate with the gods and relate their wishes.

The performance, more commonly known as the Monkey Dance, is a form of Balinese music drama that the local people developed in the 1930s. It reenacts a battle from the Ramayana in which the monkey-like Vanara helped Prince Rama fight off the evil King Ravana.

This was by far the most exotic and intriguing performance I have ever seen. The setting alone was almost dreamlike. I could not imagine having a more exotic experience as I sat under a clear, bright, star-filled sky in the middle of the jungle. Members of the French Navy were in the audience wearing their starched white shorts and white knee socks. Candles and torches lighted the entire area.

I wrote in my journal that night that I had been feeling sick and was sure that it was a lack of vitamins since our diet consisted of only rice...but then found out my problem was much, much worse.

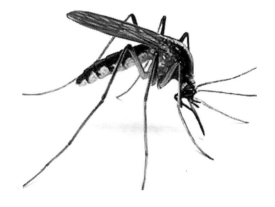

CHAPTER THRITY EIGHT
Malaria
April 5, 1959

In the middle of the night I awakened, shaking uncontrollably. I put on two sweaters, piled several other items of clothing on top of my sleeping bag, and still could not get warm. My teeth were chattering so hard that I wished that someone could hold onto me to keep me from shaking. I even considered getting in bed with Gloria.

I awakened again at 4 a.m. in a terrific sweat and was suffering with a splitting headache. My fever was so high that I was delirious. I can remember holding up a hand and watching, fascinated, as the sweat dripped from the tip of each finger, drop by drop. The headache became unbearable despite the fact that I was taking eight aspirin a day.

I was no longer able to join the student outings. Gloria and I decided to go into Denpasar and seek help from a doctor.

Right here my journal entries stop all together. I was so sick that I could not write and doubted that I would survive.

When we finally found a doctor in the city, we discovered that Gloria's German was thankfully fluent enough to communicate with the Dutch-speaking physician, as the two languages have many similarities. He diagnosed my illness as double-malaria – in fact I had two strains of the disease simultaneously. Each type occurred every other day and since I had attacks every day, I was harboring two strains. He prescribed Malaquin, a British quinine pill, and I returned to the hostel and to bed.

I really am not sure how long I was so sick; I guess about a week. We eventually returned to Bandung where I was able to recover my strength and continue the journey home.

Little did I know that this illness would impose restrictions on me for the rest of my life; many years later when I tried to give blood I learned that I could never do so having had malaria.

The most embarrassing outcome of my bout with malaria was many years later when I had an appointment for a pre-marital blood test with a doctor who was a good friend. He carefully explained that I should not be shocked if the test came back positive for syphilis, as this was often the case in former malaria patients. Fortunately, the test was fine…and I had no reason to worry anyway.

We eventually rolled back into the Bandung railroad station with me many pounds lighter and much the worse for wear. Because of the crowds celebrating the Muslim holiday Ramadan, train officials had taken special precautions before allowing our train to pass over the rebel-infested mountains near Bandung. A car loaded with armed military preceded the train, dispersing scouts to check for possible sabotage. It was not until two months later, when this same train was derailed by guerillas killing 130 persons, that we fully appreciated the added precautions.

The Bancroft's home was once again our haven for the next 10 days. We were very sad when we left that beautiful place;

not only were we leaving our friends behind but our wonderful soul mate (and fourth for bridge), Jane, who was staying on another month with her family.

There was considerable excitement awaiting us when we returned to Jakarta for the rest our trip. We reached the airport and found that our scheduled flight – a special Indian Airlines plane carrying 19 top red Chinese brass including General Yang, the Commander of the Red Army – had been forced to land in Singapore because of engine trouble.

Several hours and a few gimlets (gin and lime juice) later we saw the general and his cohorts smile their way through a long receiving line of Indonesian officials who had been waiting at least six hours for that pleasure. When the preliminaries were over, a shining caravan of Fords and Chevrolets whisked away the still smiling general and his friends.

According to our plane crew (who all bore red stars for valiant achievement on their chests), the esteemed general had not been smiling in Singapore. He refused to leave the plane so that they could make repairs. When they finally managed to remove him after four hours, he told them he would not take the substituted Malayan charter plane until an Indian Airlines official agreed to fly to Jakarta with him.

CHAPTER THIRTY NINE
Crossing the Pacific
May 21, 1959

Gloria, Sue and I flew from Bandung to Singapore and on to Hong Kong, surely one of the most dynamic and beautiful cities in the world. In fact, when friends asked about my favorite city my answer was always Hong Kong, following my negative description of Jakarta.

This jewel-like city is located in the South China Sea at the mouth of the Pearl River Delta. The name means "fragrant harbor" and is one of the deepest natural maritime ports in the world. Its name derives from the area around Aberdeen on Hong Kong Island where they traded fragrant wood products and incense. Its natural beauty is breath taking. The hills and mountainous area ascends steeply from sea level to more than 3,000 feet. The entire area comprises the Kowloon Peninsula and 263 islands.

The weather was perfect, a welcome relief from the heat
and humidity we had suffered in Indonesia. We were able to
walk up and down the steep hills in comfort. We saw all the
fascinating points of interest and did so mostly on foot –
because by this time our funds were very, very sparse. I especially
remember visiting the beautiful Tiger Balm Gardens, a public
space that no longer exists in Hong Kong. The Aw family built
the garden with the intention of promoting the Tiger Balm
products, a blend of herbal ingredients that relieve pain.

We took the tram to Victoria Peak, a funicular railway that
carried us almost 2,000 feet to the summit, where we enjoyed a
spectacular view of Victoria Harbor. We took the ferry across
to the Peninsula and visited Kowloon, where we ate on a junk
in the harbor. At the end of each day we were completely
exhausted and usually returned to our hostel early and skipped
dinner to save money. We only spent a few days in Hong
Kong, but we savored every minute of that time.

We flew from Hong Kong to Japan where we toured briefly
and even had the opportunity to ride on the famous bullet train.
We finally boarded the USS President Wilson, an American
Presidents Line ship, in Yokohama – where we reunited with
Stewart who joined us for the final leg of the journey. By
this time, we were anxious to get home. We were especially
looking forward to being on the ship where we did not have
to worry about navigation, mechanical failures or infestations
of any kind.

We made a brief stop in Honolulu Hawaii after crossing
the International Date Line (which added a 17th day to the
trip, much to our dismay). In the brief 24-hour stop, we went
for a walk on the beach and had a nice swim, but we were so
focused on getting home and seeing our families that even a
place as beautiful as Hawaii was hard to enjoy.

Because we were travelling steerage class, they did not
permit us to share any of the amenities of first class passengers
such as swimming pools, games, etc. Therefore the voyage

became much more monotonous than enjoyable. We played endless games of bridge while we listened to the clacking of the tiles from the Mahjong games of our fellow Chinese passengers.

During our brief stopover in Honolulu, I joined my uncle's sister for dinner on her cruise ship, a meal that I savored more than any other before or since. The opulence of the food selection overwhelmed me; I could barely get my fill of all the exotic foods.

When we approached the California coast and slowly passed under the Golden Gate Bridge, I had a lump in my throat and tears running down my cheeks. My return to the U.S. was as emotional an experience as my departure had been. I had just spent more than a year on the most incredible adventure of my lifetime, but to be home in the United States was a wonderful feeling.

I rode a Greyhound Bus from San Francisco to Los Angeles, the only transportation I could afford. My aunt, who lived in Beverly Hills, met me at the downtown bus depot…which I imagine was quite a shock to her – running into all the dregs of society that hung out in that part of downtown L.A.

I eventually returned to New Jersey after several weeks of rest and recovery in warm, sunny southern California. I enjoyed the fresh oranges picked from my aunt's tree and many trips to well-known restaurants. I made a smooth transition back into my real world.

I eventually secured a job with the United States Life Insurance Company in New York as a member of their public relations staff. I "switched careers" because they paid more than the newspaper business, which I would really have much preferred.

Sadly, Gloria passed away a little more than a year after our return. She had contracted a rare disease that I later learned was Myasthenia Gravis, a neuromuscular disorder. We completely lost touch with Jane, but Sue and I still exchange Christmas cards – she lives in Northern California and has two adult children and several grandchildren. I recently visited with her

in her home and we were thrilled to see each other again.
We reminisced about our fantastic adventures and agreed that
we were probably the gutsiest people we know, and were glad
we had lived to tell the tale. Sue is still the bright, cheery person
I traveled with so many years ago.

We regretted that we had lost touch with Jane when we
remembered her and her lovely family who had taken such
good care of us.

Many years after returning, I was in New York City, and
phoned Stewart at his penthouse apartment. I had been able
to track him down through stories in Time Magazine about
his truck farm where he raised vegetables on a rooftop next
to his penthouse. I identified myself but he had no interest
in seeing me or in renewing our friendship. I often read news
stories about Stewart describing his unusual activities such as
riding a bicycle to work in the city. He supported many liberal
causes and was an offbeat philanthropist. They also cited him
for maintaining unusual residences, including a Chinese junk in
New York Harbor that eventually sank. Stewart passed away in
2008 at the age of 70 from cancer.

Several months after I came home I realized that I was
not in love with Max and so with a very heavy heart, I sadly
returned his engagement ring. I knew what pain I would cause
this nice man and found this to be one of the most difficult
tasks of my life.

By then, though, I knew that the only man I loved and
could imagine spending the rest of my life with was a man who
had been a good friend for several years and with whom I had
exchanged letters throughout the trip. Dave had spent many
long hours visiting my sister while I was gone and the two of
them decided that we should marry. I guess they were right, as
our wedding took place in Morristown, New Jersey in September
of 1959 and we have lived happily ever after.

The End